For Those Who Come After

FOR THOSE WHO COME AFTER

A Study of Native American Autobiography

by Arnold Krupat

University of California Press

BERKELEY / LOS ANGELES / LONDON

University of California Press
Berkeley and Los Angeles, California
University of California Press, Ltd.
London, England
Copyright © 1985 by The Regents of the University of California

Library of Congress Cataloging in Publication Data
Krupat, Arnold.
For those who come after.
Bibliography: p.
Includes index.
1. Indians of North America—Biography.   2. Autobiography.
I. Title.
E89.5.K78   1985   973'.0497022 [B]   84-8688
ISBN 0-520-05307-9

Printed in the United States of America

1 2 3 4 5 6 7 8 9

TITLE PAGE ILLUSTRATION
Thomas Hart, Yellow Wolf, and L. V. McWhorter, October, 1908.
Courtesy of the Historical Photographs Collection of Washington
State University Libraries, Pullman, Washington.

For Cynthia, Jeremy, and Tanya

For David Brumble and Brian Swann

I thought I would write down and tell you all these things so that those who came after me would not be deceived.

CRASHING THUNDER

. . . criticism must think of itself as life-enhancing and constitutively opposed to every form of tyranny, domination, and abuse: its social goals are noncoercive knowledge produced in the interests of human freedom.

EDWARD SAID

Contents

Preface

Of the many different types of autobiographical documents produced by Native American people, this book focuses on one—what I shall call the Indian autobiography. Constituted as a genre of writing by the principle of original, bicultural, composite composition, Indian autobiographies are not a traditional form among Native peoples but the consequence of contact with the white invader-settlers, and the product of a limited collaboration with them. Both their production and their function involve complex, cross-cultural issues, issues in their particulars quite familiar to the linguist, the anthropologist, and the historian. An adequate reading of these texts requires consideration of the language, culture, and history both of Native Americans and of Euramericans; yet, I will contend, such a reading must be centrally a *literary* reading—one, however, which can as well be carried out by the linguist, anthropologist, or historian as by the professional specialist in literature, all of whom, I believe, are equally partners in the practice of social science.

My own training and academic experience happen to be specifically literary, and, in what follows, I try to provide literary readings of several nineteenth- and twentieth-century Indian autobiographies that are exemplary—although not in a rigorously systematic way—of that "Approach" to Native American texts I describe in the opening chapter.

The texts chosen for study were not chosen in any random fashion nor because of their status as apparent "classics" of their genre. Nor have I attempted to survey or "cover" the field; indeed, if I had, the absence, for example, of detailed analyses of the autobiographies of Native American women—which I regret, in any case—would have been simply unconscionable. Rather, the texts I chose were those that allowed me most readily to show (1) their relation to their historical period, (2) their relation to the discursive categories of history, science, and art (literature), and (3) their relation to the four modes of emplotment—romance, tragedy, comedy, irony—by which Western authors (or editors) must structure narrative. I would be pleased if the reader found the four areas of my "Approach" and these three particular relationships suggestive of ways to study the many other Indian autobiographies inevitably neglected here.

Native American literary composition both oral and written has not yet entered the canon of American literature and has not, for that reason, attracted the attention of our many current theorists of literature. For new movements in critical theory generally seek to establish themselves by strong readings of the canonical texts—which texts, thus newly illuminated, have their canonical status reaffirmed. Given this relation between new critical directions and the Eurocentric, standard, canon of American literature, it is easy to see why Native American literatures have not been set in the light of a wide range of advanced perspectives. Unfortunately, it must be said that those who do study Native American literatures have thus far tended to avoid critical theory as if it were indeed the French disease, a foreign corruption hostile or irrelevant to their local efforts. The theorists have thus missed out on some extraordinary opportunities to test and apply their ideas, while the literary pragmatists—to call them that—have permitted themselves to carry on at some virtually pretechnological level of critical naiveté; the amount of unself-conscious twaddle about plots and characters and the poetry of place that goes on at the literary end of Native American studies would never be tolerated in the study of, say, Faulkner or William Carlos Williams, of Emily Dickinson or Thoreau. It should not be tolerated in the study of Indian literatures; and it is one of the purposes of this book to effect some small degree of rapprochement between the two separate camps of theorists and Native Americanists who have kept their distance from one another at some considerable price to each.

Some of these essays have appeared before, in slightly different or in briefer form. I am grateful to *Critical Inquiry* for permission to reprint "An Approach to Native American Texts" (vol. 9, no. 2, December 1982); to *American Literature* for "The Indian Autobiography: Origins, Type, and Function" (vol. 53, no. 1, March 1981, copyright 1981 by the Duke University Press); and to Willis Regier and the University of Nebraska Press for parts of "The Case of Crashing Thunder," which appeared as Introduction and Appendix to Paul Radin's *Crashing Thunder: The Autobiography of an American Indian* (copyright 1983 by the University of Nebraska Press).

My intellectual debts are abundantly documented in the notes, but there are particular and substantial debts beyond what can be noted to the work of Roy Harvey Pearce, Edward Said, Raymond Williams, and Marvin Harris: their writing has been inspiration, pleasure, encouragement, and goad.

I work out of a small liberal arts college, not an ancient or extended university; without the ongoing and active help of the Sarah Lawrence librarians—in particular, Phyllis Byan, now retired—I could not have obtained the many texts I needed to see. Their efficient and generous help at every stage of research I wish gratefully to acknowledge.

Edwin Cady, editor of *American Literature,* worked with me on my first attempt to say something about Indian autobiography. His editorial "statement," as Huck Finn says, "was interesting but tough,"—persistent, and always challenging, too. In everything I have tried to do since, I have sought to meet his standards of clarity and integrity.

Robert von Hallberg of *Critical Inquiry* provided insightful commentary and advice on the initial, theoretical essay of the book, and Mary Caraway of the *Critical Inquiry* staff took some of the lumps out of some awkward prose. I am grateful to both of them.

The anthropologists Stanley Diamond, Irving Goldman, and, most particularly, Nancy O. Lurie graciously read and commented on early drafts of my study of *Crashing Thunder.* Whatever they may think of it now, I am much indebted to them.

Phyllis Sangenito typed and retyped the manuscript, for which I thank her.

And I am most fortunate to have worked with Stanley Holwitz, a fellow New Yorker, though a deserter from the eccentric Apple; he has "handled" this manuscript from early to late with tact and good humor.

Finally, I want to acknowledge the polymorphous help— distracting yet sustaining—of my family to whom this book is dedicated, as well as the support of my colleagues and friends, Brian Swann and David Brumble, to whom it is also dedicated: without them, family and friends, nothing.

A. K.

New York, 1984

For Those Who Come After

1/

An Approach to

Native American Texts

Critical commentary on Native American literature dates virtually from the very moment of its "discovery" by Euramericans, a discovery which perhaps did not occur until the second quarter of the nineteenth century. But the earliest students of Indian literatures had little in the way of sound cultural and linguistic data on which to base their understanding. It was probably not until the twentieth century, the result, largely, of the work of Franz Boas and his students, that an approximately accurate scientific knowledge of the many Native languages and cultures of America began

Manuscript page of Sam Blowsnake's (Crashing Thunder's) autobiography in the Winnebago syllabary. From the Paul Radin papers, courtesy of the American Philosophical Society Library, Philadelphia, Pennsylvania.

to be achieved. And it is only since the 1950s that structural analysis of Native literatures, spurred by Lévi-Strauss's work on "myth," has made much progress.

Lévi-Strauss's binary method of analysis opposed the "myth" to the "poem," the first infinitely translatable, the second virtually untranslatable. In Lévi-Strauss's work, much of what might be considered the literature of "primitive" people is treated as myth, its content available for transformation into abstract pairs while its form, its actual language and performative dynamics, is largely ignored or dismissed.

Dell Hymes contributed significantly to the study of Native American texts by producing the conceptual structures of Native American narratives as a function of their particular linguistic structures, thus accepting Lévi-Strauss's insistence on their broad meaningfulness while rejecting his indifference to the actual terms of their presentation. Hymes has recently reminded us of what should have been obvious all along, that "the problems of understanding what Native American narrators have intended and expressed is difficult enough. It is far more difficult if, in a certain sense, we do not know what they said."[1] In all too many cases it is not possible to "know what they said," for what they said was never transcribed—or if transcribed, not preserved. All the more reason, then, to pay particularly close attention to those transcriptions (and, more recently, tapes) which do exist. Hymes himself, unusually learned in Native languages, has shown how informed scrutiny of transcriptions can reveal structural patterns which had been entirely obscured in English prose translation.

Beyond the considerable difficulty of knowing "what they said" lies the difficulty of knowing how they said it. For

[2]

Native American literature presents itself exclusively in the form of oral performances, not textual objects; no matter how scrupulous a transcription may be, it is inevitably a declension from the narrative as act.

Recent developments in poststructuralism, whatever their effect on the reading of Western literature, have had an enormously salutary effect on the reading of Native American literature. With the reexamination of such concepts as voice, text, and performance, and of the ontological and epistemological status of the sign, has come a variety of effective means for specifying and demonstrating the complexity and richness of Native American literature. Attempting to recuperate the performative dimension, Dennis Tedlock worked directly from tape recordings to produce his well-known anthology from the Zuni, *Finding the Center* (1972). Tedlock used typographical variations to convey changes of pitch, volume, and pace; he also indicated the audience responses important to Native American narrative. Tedlock is perhaps foremost among those students of Indian literature wishing to move "toward an oral poetics."[2]

Although it seems the case that our textual culture is presently restructuring itself to replace print with the printout, moving, in Father Walter Ong's phrase, to the "secondary orality of the electronic age,"[3] I still do not think we are likely to develop an "oral poetics." The concept of an oral poetics nonetheless remains important as a check to the Euramerican tendency to project alphabetic categories onto the nonalphabetic practice of Native Americans. We need to acknowledge the (very nearly disabling) fact that most of us (non-Indians, but a great many Indians, too) are going to experience Native American literary art almost

[3]

exclusively in textual form. No matter how the type is sized or arranged on the page, it will be, in Gayatri Spivak's phrase, the "graphic of the trace" that we encounter, not the presence of the voice.[4] Yet we need to acknowledge as well that our desire for lost originals here is not the nostalgia of Western metaphysics but the price of Western imperial history. It is as a result of the conquest and dispossession of the tribes that the signifier replaces the act; our script marked on the page is the pale trace of what their voices performed. There is, nonetheless, every reason to attempt to understand the texts we have and to try to imagine the performances we have lost (some of them the better imagined because of the tape recordings of performances which we do have).

There has been a sufficient amount of sophisticated writing about Native American literature in the last ten years or so to constitute a New Indian Criticism. In the remainder of this chapter, I want to move in the direction of a systematization by examining the concepts of (1) the mode of production of the text, (2) the author, (3) literature, and (4) canonicity to show how they can be organized into an approach to Native American texts.

The Mode of Production of the Text

The concept of the mode of production—which includes the forces or means of production and the relations of production—derives from Marxist studies in which it designates the particular form of a given society's economic organization at a given time. Because the mode of production— the economic base—is considered largely to determine social relationships, and social relationships to determine consciousness and its material expressions, the importance of the mode of production to literary studies—part of the superstructure of culture, law, religion, and the like—is clear. This is, of course, to assert what should be apparent but in a great deal of American liberal criticism is not—that texts are social and material, that they are made actively and by the expenditure of labor, and that they are commodities whose exchange value is not solely a question of the economics of publishing.

Important as this is for Euramerican writing, it is absolutely crucial for Native American texts, which cannot even be thought except as the products of a complex but historically specifiable division of labor. There simply were no Native American texts until whites decided to collaborate with Indians and make them. Nor is it unworthy of mention that they did not decide to make them until the late nineteenth century, when the American economy itself had shifted its base to making. Earlier, in the colonial period, trade was economically paramount. From the Revolutionary period into the nineteenth century, America's wealth was based upon cultivation, not production: agri-culture and land "improvement" were, in Benjamin Franklin's phrase, "the way to wealth." So long as this remained the case, Revolutionaries and Americans defined themselves against the Indian as wholly other. They insisted, despite abundant evidence to the contrary, that the Natives were hunters, not farmers, and as noncultivators could have no culture—thus nothing worthy of textualization.

Although the earliest translation-version of an Indian "poem" dates from the American Revolutionary period, with few exceptions Indian texts did not begin to be produced until the 1830s, when the eastern tribes were forcibly removed west of the Mississippi. It was then that Indians, still popularly believed to have no culture of their own and so no capacity for cultural contribution, were accorded a history—one which began when a particular tribe resisted white encroachment. Indian resistance was not new, having commenced almost at the first moment of white invasion; what was new after 1830 was an interest in the Indians' own perspective on this "history." This led to the development of the Indian autobiography as an attempt to preserve, complete, or correct the record in the name of historical justice. But most of what appears today in the anthologies of Indian literature—poems, tales, stories, and the like—was collected after the Civil War, very roughly from 1887 to 1934, inscribed by anthropologists determined to preserve this vanishing heritage in the name of science.

The rigorously trained workers sent into the field by Franz Boas after the turn of the century, conscious of their status as scientists, valued "translations that were 'direct' or 'close' or 'literal,'" as Tedlock has noted. These they "published with as few changes as possible from the sort of English used by interpreters or bilingual narrators."[5] This procedure led inevitably to the sort of "disaster" Tedlock quotes from Elsie Clews Parsons and Ruth Benedict. Frank Hamilton Cushing and other field workers, however, who preceded Boas's students and who defined their scientific mission more loosely, seem to have erred in a different direction, achieving a "style," in Tedlock's estimate, "more Victorian than Indian."[6] If the anthropological scientists produced either a florid "Victorian" style or a stiff, wooden style rather than an "Indian" style, what of the poets and humanists who have tried their hand at producing an Indian literature?

Early in this century, Mary Austin admitted her role in the production of the signifier by calling the Indian poems

[6]

in her anthology, *The American Rhythm*, "reëxpressions" of Amerindian songs.[7] That their style owes as much to imagist free verse as to "Indian" style is obvious, however, and the obvious result of Austin's contribution. More recently, William Brandon and, particularly, Jerome Rothenberg have extensively revised, even rewritten, Indian materials, thereby claiming to have achieved a more authentic Indian version than literal transcription and translation could provide. But it is difficult to avoid concluding once more that "Indian" style (whatever one conceives it to be) has been lost to the inscriber's cultural allegiance: Rothenberg's Indian poems appear, we may say, in postmodernist or *Alcheringa* style.[8]

But this is why the concept of the mode of production is of such importance, for it forces us to go beyond any given editor's account of (or silence in regard to) how a text was made in the direction of historical reconstruction. Indian texts are always the consequence of a collaboration, and, no matter what we wish to say about them, it is useful to know, as far as we can, just how they were made. How many workers, for example, were involved in the production of the final text, and what did each contribute to it? Do variants of a given version exist, and, if so, what were the differences in the production of each? How well did the various workers (Indian informant-speaker, white editor-transcriber, and also apparently in all cases at least one translator, usually part-Indian and part-white) know one another's language? Under what auspices was the text produced, and what claims were made for it? Was its inscription sponsored by anthropological science and, if so, through a museum or a university? Was it paid for by the government or by a private individual? Was it sponsored historically or legally, in relation to a particular event or a particular claim? Was it sponsored poetically, religiously, morally, or in the interest of revitalizing some aspect of American practice? What were the apparent intentions of the producers and what benefits did they derive from their collaborative project?

To augment the empirical dimension such considerations hope to provide, we need also at least raise the question of publication, distribution, and reception—thus to introduce, as it were, Pierre Macherey (*A Theory of Literary Production*) to William Charvat (*The Profession of Authorship in America, 1800–1870*). Clearly texts published by major commercial houses, and advertised in and reviewed by large-circulation journals or periodicals, make their way differently and with different effectivity from texts brought out by small, specialized, or private presses and not widely reviewed or publicized. In "The Shaping of a Canon: U.S. Fiction, 1960–1975," Richard Ohmann has begun to explore the many apparently extraliterary factors that determine whether a novel will find a place on the American "cultural agenda."[9] Parallel, if not strictly equivalent, factors operate in the case of Native American texts, and those of us interested in these texts will have to ask not only more searching theoretical but more precisely focused socioempirical questions about them.

If questions like these seem uninteresting, I can only say that they are necessary so far as we aspire to some degree of rigorous understanding. If questions like these seem unliterary, I can only say that it is precisely on their answers that any judgment of literariness will depend. Inquiry into the mode of production of most of the Native American texts conventionally studied as "scientific"—historical or anthropological—reveals complexities that seem far more

accurately comprehended by a specifically literary herme-
neutics. (The converse might also turn out to be true: thus
the work of Hyemeyohsts Storm which presents itself as
fiction might better be studied for its sociological or anthropological interest.) Jack Goody's observation that "most
transcription transforms, often in complex ways; one can
never be quite sure what utterance the 'text' represents,"
returns us to Hymes's concern for what Native American
narrators actually said and marks the point of departure for
the kind of work that must be done for Native texts.[10] Whatever Native American narrators may have said and however
they may have said it, we will begin to understand what we
have only when we recognize that the signifier's complex
composition is the result of a historically specifiable mode
of production—the result not only of the confrontation of
two individuals, but equally, in Fredric Jameson's words,
"the confrontation of two distinct social forms or modes of
production," a collective as well as an individual encounter.[11]

The Author

All texts are materially produced, but not all texts have
authors. Michel Foucault notes that:

> . . . a private letter may have a signatory, but it does not have
> an author; a contract can have an underwriter, but not an
> author; and, similarly, an anonymous poster attached to a wall
> may have a writer, but he cannot be an author. In this sense,
> the function of an author is to characterize the existence, cir-
> culation, and operation of certain discourses within a society.[12]

Foucault's statement has bearing upon the types and categories of use or exchange of any "discourse" and upon its

consequent valuation: American Indian discourse, until very recently, has been notoriously lacking in its possession of named authors, and this has assuredly contributed to Euramerican neglect of it. As Foucault also notes, "Discourse that possesses an author's name is not to be immediately consumed and forgotten; neither is it accorded the momentary attention given to ordinary, fleeting words. Rather, its status and its manner of reception are regulated by the culture in which it circulates."[13] But can one attach an author's name to American Indian discourse? And, if so, whose? For its "status and its manner of reception" have always been tied to its presumptive anonymity, its lack of named authors.

In European and Euramerican culture, the rise of the author parallels the rise of the individual. Homologous with the bourgeois conceptualization of an opposition between the individual and society appears the corollary opposition between individual (private) and collective (public) production and composition. Individual composition means written composition, for only texts can have individual authors. From the eighteenth century forward, individual authors are protected by copyright laws. Authors are—the idea would seem to be obvious—the individual creators of the individual works which carry their names; accordingly, they are fully entitled to profit from the sale and circulation of their private property.

With the development of the conception of individual authorship, half of the etymological sense of the word *author*, previously strong in ordinary understanding, dropped out of currency. "Author" is from the Latin *augere*, which means both "to originate" and "to augment." But from the eighteenth and, most particularly, from the nineteenth century on, authors were regarded strictly as originators. Not Milton's desire to augment the tradition of elegy or epic, nor Pope's to say well what's oft been thought, but the will to original creation came to dominate literary projects. The author-ity of the author, in this view, derives not from his predecessors and their productions, nor from his contemporaries and theirs, but, instead, from his personality, his imagination or, arriving at the ultimate mystification, from his individual genius which transcends the society that would seek to constrain it.

This particular mythology never developed in Native American culture, where the individual who spoke only for himself spoke, therefore, for no one else; where the individual could not in any positive way be imagined to stand outside or against his society; where, as generations of whites lamented, there was an utterly deficient appreciation of the virtues of private property; and where, of course, there was no writing—and so no authors.

In studying this situation, John Bierhorst has spoken of the essential "anonymity" of Indian literature, for "the Indian poet does not consider himself the originator of his material but merely the conveyor. Either he has heard it from an elder or he has received it from a supernatural power. . . . Indian poetry, then, is usually attributed not to an individual but to his culture."[14]

But even this does not quite get it right, inasmuch as it is founded on a dichotomy (if not an actual opposition) between the individual and society/culture. Each successive performance of traditional material "conveys" that material, to be sure, but it is never purely a repetition of it. For, as

Dennis Tedlock explains the situation among the Zuni, the "conveyer" is always an "interpreter" as well:

> . . . [and] the interpreter may suddenly realize something or understand something for the first time on this particular occasion. The teller is not merely repeating memorized words; nor is he or she merely giving a dramatic "oral interpretation" or "concert reading" of a fixed script. We are in the presence of a *performing art*, all right, but we are getting the *criticism* at the same time and from the same person.[15]

Howard Norman has recently published translations of a Swampy Cree trickster cycle—but the contemporary narrators of this traditional material produce narratives that are, finally, substantially *original*. Theirs is the originality of augmentation, not of pure origination. (This roughly parallels differences between various Native creation tales, where even in "the beginning" something always already exists, and the Judeo-Christian creation story in Genesis, which presents the absolute origination of the world through the solitary activity of God, the Author of Creation.)[16]

This posed a considerable dilemma for those who wished to write Indian "literature." What was the Euramerican who published Indian poems to call himself? He was not their author, for he did not originate the material, and he could not admit to having augmented it without provoking the charge that he had thereby contaminated its authenticity. He was not merely the translator, for translators work from texts (sometimes in consultation with authors) and usually claim full competency in the language from which they are translating. Indian literature is not textual, and, to my knowledge, virtually no Euramerican translator has ever tried to work entirely on the basis of his own competence in the Native language. Referring to oneself as the editor evades none of these problems, for the question arises, what editorial principle guided the final production of the text?

In the name of scientific accuracy, the late nineteenth- and early twentieth-century students of Boas, as I have noted, aimed for literalness in their translations, and contemporary commentators like William Bevis approve this commitment to "what they said." Poets from Austin to Rothenberg, in contrast, have tended to see literalness as a bar to authenticity in translation. To get the actual feel of the thing (as they imagine it to have felt), they have taken great liberties in translation, seeking, in general, to convey "how they said it." Tedlock, at present, speaks well of this procedure.

On the basis of recent work, it seems reasonable to require that translations from Native American literature, if they are to be considered approximately authentic, meet two conditions. First, they must derive from an actual, taped, or re-creative audition of the Native performance. Second, they must be produced in accord with what Dell Hymes has called "philological recognition of the original, not bilingual control," at least a fair working knowledge of the language in question.[17] But even when translators meet these two conditions, they may still present the "same" song or story, in writing and in English, in very different forms. (This is, of course, what happens to some degree with all translations.) Native American texts regularly present a case analogous to what Frank Kermode describes as necessitating a choice between the search (vain, as Kermode thinks) for what the text "originally meant" and what it "originally means"—except that in Native American literature not just the meaning but the very text itself is always in question.[18]

However we may seek to resolve this sort of problem, the poststructuralist movement away from binary procedures should at least make it familiar, indeed even attractive, to consider. For Native American texts present concrete and actual instances of a kind that must remain hypothetical— however vigorously argued—within Western writing. E. D. Hirsch probably remains the most vigorous defender of the author and his intentions as the ethically and esthetically privileged determinators of the text and its meaning, while Norman Holland and Stanley Fish claim that only the reader's activity constitutes the text. Critics as widely diverse as Raymond Williams and Wolfgang Iser have attempted to reconcile these opposed contentions. All of this, of course, bears upon our understanding of "author," and our understanding can be advanced by attention to Native American practice.

As Hymes writes:

> Comparative study of Native American narratives and analysis of fine individual narratives together make evident, behind the many varied linkages, shapings, and realizations of plots and motifs, the working of many reflective and articulate minds. In our own culture we would call such working with the received materials of our literary tradition authorship. We should do so in the case of Native Americans as well . . . in order to do justice to their accomplishments. But the notion, "author," is ours, not theirs.[19]

This seems just: yet "our" present "notion" of authorship has begun to describe something not so very different from "their" practice. We have come to recognize, for example, that even in our literature the force and authority of individual texts derives from what Edward Said has called a system of "affiliation . . . an often implicit network of peculiarly cultural . . . associations between forms, statements, and other aesthetic elaborations on the one hand, and on the other, institutions, agencies, classes, and fairly amorphous social forces."[20]

One way to specify some of the common problematics of Euramerican and Native American texts is to add to Jameson's reminder that their mode of production is collective the observation made by Raymond Williams that each of these texts is nonetheless an "individual project" as well. For "the irreducibly individual projects that particular works are, may come in experience and in analysis to show resemblances which allow us to group them into collective modes."[21]

From this perspective we can see not only that the vaunted autonomy of the author in Western literature is not total but also that the anonymity of the Native American "conveyor" is not total either. We must not let the look of our writing entirely obscure for us the fact that it too is, in Kenneth Burke's still serviceable term, "dramatistic," a performance in which not only language but the human voice speaks, a voice at once individual and collective. In the same way, Indian narrators in successive performances do not only "convey" but comment, adding, deleting, and supplying emphases that alter as well as merely reproduce the already given.[22] We can see, therefore, that the Indian collective-anonymous "author" and the bourgeois individual-named "author" are not so much opposites as variants of

[15]

the exercise of what (in Foucault's phrase) we may call the "author-function." But if this is so, we will have to think of literature as something other than the pure creation of the great author.

Literature

The term *literature* today is undergoing a transformation as a result of two interrelated though very different developments. The first of these—that within advanced academic criticism—is fairly easy to describe and perhaps largely complete. The second of these—that within the technology of microcomputers—is not so clear and probably only in its early stages. Though it exceeds the scope of our study, I may say that the shift from the page to the screen, from the library to the computer bank, is a real revolution; we are in the midst of a change to a genuinely new mode of production.

At present in America, critics like Harold Bloom and the late Paul de Man have expanded the specific nineteenth-century meaning of literature as "expressive and imaginative writing" to include all writing, thus causing the older, etymological force of literature (from *littera*, letter) to reemerge. All writing is imaginative and expressive, it has been claimed, after Derrida, because of the illimitable free play of signification inherent in the act of inscription itself, what de Man calls "the proliferating and disruptive power of figural language."[23] Yet the figural simply cannot be purged from writing; philosophers and social scientists cannot produce texts safe from figural disruption and self-deconstruction; neither, of course, can literary critics, whose texts, to use Bloom's terminology, are in any case misreadings or "misprisions" precisely as they are "strong" readings. Thus we are to believe that all writing is literature in the nineteenth-century sense merely, as in the older etymological sense, by being writing.

Indians, of course, did not write—at least they had no alphabet and marked no letters on paper. Perhaps, as Lewis Henry Morgan would conclude, they had risen above the level of "savagery," yet they remained "barbarians," analphabetically short of the supreme condition of "civilization."[24] Literature, product of the man of letters—poet, philosopher, historian, or divine—clearly could not exist among the culture-less, uncivilized children of nature, who did not write. When Thomas Jefferson, in a famous example, quoted the speech of Chief Logan, his purpose was to assert the rationality and intelligence of Indians by showing them capable of eloquent oratory; but this was still deemed antecedent to a capacity for writing and for *litterature.*

By the early nineteenth century, literature came to mean not the entire culture of letters but, particularly, imaginative and expressive utterance—in writing, to be sure, but also, as Wordsworth noted, in the speech of common men who might not be able to write. Romanticism's discovery of the "organic" Middle Ages (a period increasingly attractive as English society, industrializing, came to be considered "mechanical"), gave rise to an expanded awareness of oral literature as something other than a contradiction in terms. Once these ideas crossed the ocean, it became attractive (at least in the East) to think of Indians as standing in for America's missing feudal past, to hear their chants as poetic (rather than as satanic, or as gibberish), as constituting a

[17]

literature that remained only to be established in writing. Although men like the Moravian Father John Heckewelder began this task even before the time of Indian Removal, very little was actually achieved until the last quarter of the nineteenth century when, as I have noted, most of what we find in the anthologies of Indian literature today was collected by anthropologists engaged in the practice of science. As the concept of the frontier yielded to that of the fieldwork, first the anthropologists of the Bureau of American Ethnology and the newly founded museums, and then the wave of anthropologists trained by Boas set out to preserve the material and ceremonial (but not the social and political) culture of the "vanishing race." Daniel Brinton, James Mooney, Alice Fletcher, Frances Densmore, Alfred Kroeber, Paul Radin, Robert Lowie, Parsons, Cushing, Boas himself, and others collected, recorded, transcribed, and translated—and some of what they got was considered literature.

These first recorders—to whom, whatever their limitations, we owe an enormous debt—had no uniform system of nomenclature for describing and cataloging the different materials they recorded, nor have we yet made much progress in this area. Horatio Hale, in 1883, published *The Iroquois Book of Rites*, which included compositions we might well call literature. Brinton, in 1890, published "Native American Poetry"; Cushing produced his *Outlines of Zuni Creation Myths* in 1896, and in 1901 materials he thought better described as *Zuni Folk Tales*. Fletcher thought she had got *Indian Story and Song from North America* (1900), and in the same year Mooney published *Myths of the Cherokees*, to follow his earlier *Sacred Formulas of the Cherokees* (1891). Edward Sapir simply used the term *text* for his *Takelma Texts* of 1909, something Boas had done already by 1894 in his *Chinook Texts*; Boas also used *traditions*, *folk tales*, and *myths*. Finally, to limit this listing, Densmore's important publications from 1913 to 1939 gave us the texts and notations for what she always regarded as Chippewa, Teton Sioux, Papago, Pawnee, Nootka, and Quileute *music*.

Many of the same terms recur in works from the 1930s to the 1950s in the collections of Ruth Bunzel (1933), Ella Deloria (1932), Archie Phinney (1934) and, importantly, Melville Jacobs, who used the terms *myth*, *text*, and ultimately *oral literature* (*The Content and Style of an Oral Literature* [1959]). More recently, Hymes has used *myth*, *text*, *story*, and *poem*; Tedlock's dissertation concerns *The Ethnography of Tale-Telling at Zuni* (1968), although his *Finding the Center* collects *Narrative Poetry of the Zuni Indians*. Rothenberg subtitles *Shaking the Pumpkin*, *Traditional Poetry of the Indian North Americas*, and in another collection he has named Indian narrators *Technicians of the Sacred*. We may conclude with a return to the general category "literature" with Jarold Ramsey's *Coyote Was Going There* (1977), an anthology of *Indian Literature of the Oregon Country*, and Karl Kroeber's collection of *Traditional American Indian Literatures: Texts and Interpretations* (1981).

Although there are presently some generally accepted criteria for distinguishing, say, a myth from a tale, there are no parallel criteria for determining whether both or neither is literature. We can gain some sense of just how complex the situation was for the anthropological collector of what might be literary materials from Margot Liberty's description of the task facing Francis La Flesche, who himself was a Native American, among the Osage:

> There were seven degrees of the Nonhonzhinga Ieta or War Rites alone, and each gens had its own version of each of the seven. (These are not well defined or known except for the first, second, and seventh: having varied in order of recitation among the various gentes; and a majority having—despite La Flesche's best efforts—rolled under "the sheet waters of oblivion" long ago.) Those collected by La Flesche, who tried to get one from at least one gens in each of the two main tribal divisions or moieties (the Tzizhu or Sky division had seven gentes, and the Honga or Earth division fourteen gentes: the latter being split into the Honga and the Wazhazhe or Osage subdivisions, of seven gentes each) ran about 100 pages each of free translation. This yielded approximately a ten percent sample of . . . the War Rites alone. . . . I am suggesting here that the Osage ceremonial record if reasonably complete in all versions of everything would run to some 40,000 pages of print, from fifty to eighty volumes of the dimensions of the typical 500–800 page Annual Report of the Bureau of American Ethnology.[25]

The temptation is great, on the one hand, to call none of this "literature" because it constitutes a "ceremonial record" of "rites"—except that a very good deal of this sort of thing has already a considerable history precisely as literature in translation. On the other hand, we might be tempted to call it all "literature," falling back upon Williams's broad definition of the word: "the process and the result of formal composition within the social and formal properties of a language."[26]

But there is another dimension to this problem we must consider before attempting a solution. The rest of this book studies Indian autobiographies almost every one of which was recorded as an historical or scientific document, not as a literary text. (I believe the distinction between the two types is important to retain for reasons that will appear later.) Because not merely their textualization but their very existence is a function of Euramerican pressure—Indian autobiographies, that is, have no precontact equivalents—these texts cannot be considered part of *traditional* Native American literature. Yet, as autobiographies, they have, in theory, as much claim to literary typology as, say, the *Confessions* of Augustine or of Cellini, or as Jonathan Edwards's *Personal Narrative*, or Benjamin Franklin's autobiography, all of which appear in anthologies and courses of *literature*.

For even if it should turn out—which I am far from granting—that most of these texts are not very good or interesting (evaluative criteria are particularly problematic, of course, and cross-cultural evaluative criteria even more so), that would still be insufficient reason for excluding them. For, in practice, the texts we teach and write about are those of a certain kind as well as of a certain quality. If Native American texts, as I shall presently argue, have claims to consideration as a literary kind, they necessarily have claims to consideration with similar texts of their kind (their quality to be judged differentially in relation to those texts).

For the Western critic to call a text of any period or culture a *literary* text is to announce a cognitively responsible decision (one for which the reasons are clearly stated or implied) to foreground the signifier. The particular concern of literary criticism, then, is texts responsibly read *as* literary in the interest of generating, by means of the literary reading, probabilistically verifiable theories or laws of a nontrivial nature. This interest makes literary criticism a branch of the social sciences, one which meets the criteria for nontrivial effectivity in about the same ways as any social science theory or law does, parsimoniously explaining much by little, and accounting for the phenomena under consideration not perfectly but at least more cogently than any prior, parallel attempt.[27] This is impossible when the composition of the signifier is treated idealistically, as *écriture*, rather than materially in relation to its mode of production, for in that case, only logical—nonempirical—operations are involved. In the forms of deconstructive practice associated not even so much with Derrida himself as with his Yale followers, de Man and J. Hillis Miller, language is taken as, synchronically, an unbounded differential system, a structure of difference and deferral with no limits to the play of signification and, diachronically, as a structure of sedimentation, where etymological and philological "history" operates but independently of any extralinguistic systems. Since mental gestures are alone involved in the critical act, probabilistic falsification is not accepted as disqualifying the results of the inquiry (e.g., Lévi-Strauss's well-known indifference to whether his schema reveal how the minds of certain natives work or only how his own mind works) which are, therefore, inevitably metaphysical or esthetic (e.g., where only misreading is possible, criticism itself becomes literature). To speak of the mode of production of the signifier is to historicize and materialize its composition and to permit comparison between the literary mode of production and the general mode of production in force at a given place and time; it is to commit oneself to the methods and goals of a sophisticated social science whose models have long ceased to derive from closed-system physics.

Whatever the historical or anthropological uses to which Native American texts may be put, the particular complexity of their mode of production seems a sufficient if not necessary reason to foreground the signifier and justify a literary reading. We note, thus, a complication in the makeup of the signifier that results not only from the nature of writing in general but from the particularities of history. But if we claim literariness for all Native American texts, we must further claim they are entitled to consideration for inclusion among the canonic texts of American literature.

Canonicity

The concept of *canon*, or tradition, can be understood in two related ways. The first is simply as that which makes the text intelligible as a discursive type. Canon, here, means roughly the same thing as genre in either its "semantic" form (the modal perspective—comedy, romance, tragedy, irony—most readily associated with Northrop Frye) or its "syntactic" form (the structural perspective of Vladimir Propp or Tzvetan Todorov's early work), to use Jameson's distinction.[28] "Genres," as Jameson points out, "are essentially literary institutions, or social contracts between a writer and a specific public, whose function is to specify the proper use of a particular cultural artifact" (Jameson, *TPU*, p. 106). But canon also can mean a selection from among genres— not merely a tradition of texts (Todorov's "fantastic" fictions, Annette Kolodny's or Nina Baym's women's domestic fictions) but the Great Tradition—those texts posited as the genuinely excellent by Matthew Arnold or F. R. Leavis, by T. S. Eliot or his violent critic, Harold Bloom. Here we must speak of the institutional or pedagogical canon.

Understood in this second sense, the canon, like all cultural production, is never an innocent selection of the best that has been thought and said; rather, it is the institutionalization of those particular verbal artifacts which appear best to convey and sustain the dominant social order.

In our own time, the canon is established primarily by the professoriate, by teacher-critics who variously—passively or actively but, for the most part—support the existing order. As Leslie Fiedler has remarked, " . . . literature is effectively what we teach in departments of English; or, conversely, what we teach in departments of English is literature."[29] Roland Barthes has offered a similar observation. "The 'teaching of literature,'" Barthes said, "is for me almost tautological. Literature is what is taught, that's all."[30] What the pedagogical canon includes from the past and from current production generally and substantially works to ratify the present and to legitimate an established hegemony by presenting what Raymond Williams calls "the *selective tradition:* that which, within the terms of an effective dominant culture, is always passed off as '*the* tradition,' '*the* significant past.'" Tradition, here, is conceived of as "an aspect of *contemporary* social and cultural organization, in the interest of the dominance of a specific class . . . a version of the past which is intended to connect with and ratify the present."[31] Any attempt to expand the canon— not merely add to it another "strong" poet but open it up to work deriving from other values—is an attempt to call into question the particular value it institutionalizes, and this (as the presently much maligned history of the 1960s shows) has important political implications.

By beginning with the mode of production of the text, I have begun at the logical theoretical beginning, but this is not the way in which most literary instruction in the schools is carried on. Rather, students commonly begin with a syllabus listing the selected texts of the canon; this identifies the great authors and defines the meaning of literature. Beyond some mention of history or biography as "background," instruction rarely moves outside the canon as a largely autonomous and self-enclosed system; any such move would run the risk of trespass on other well-fenced fields. "Every relationship of 'hegemony' is necessarily a pedagogical relation," Antonio Gramsci observed; and the "pedagogical relation" in the schools is organized to ensure that the question of the mode of production can never arise.[32]

If the mode of production of Native American texts urges that they be considered literary texts, then they must be permitted entrance into a variety of literary canons. This means that Indian literature of apparently familiar types (creation and origin stories, etiological tales, invocations and prayers, lyrics of love or mourning, etc.) must be more frequently and abundantly taught, written about, and imitated along with their European and Euramerican counterparts. This means, as well, that the great body of Native American narratives which, until quite recently, has virtually been ignored by students and critics of literature, must be examined to determine on the one hand what the appropriate generic groupings among them might be and, on the other, the relation of these genres to the familiar Western narrative types. Some Native American narratives, for example, would be interesting to study in relation to the texts of Kafka, Borges, and Barthelme, and, theoretically, as possible types of essentially nonrepresentational, nonmimetic fiction.

The inclusion of Native texts in the canon of American literature could beneficially alter the pedagogical order in the schools (which, despite the distance of contemporary theory from the post-Kantian model I have sketched, seems largely to persist); by persisting in ignoring their mode of production we do more immediate and immediately discoverable violence to Native texts than to the standard, canonic texts of the Western tradition. By working with Native American texts among other types of what Jameson has called "hitherto marginalized types of discourse," critical theory may find significant opportunities to test and refine itself in practical application (Jameson, *TPU*, p. 106). For obvious, but not necessary, reasons, our major theorists, with the important exception of Said, are entirely Eurocentric. Attention to Indian literature would help move us away from our traditional practice of isolating the components of textual objects in the direction of what Williams calls "discover[ing] the nature of a practice and then its conditions" (*Base and Superstructure*, p. 47). Here, we would not—I return to Jameson—oppose "the response of an individual subject to the collective realities of any moment of the past" or of another culture but instead establish "the quite different relationship of an objective situation in the present with an objective situation in the past."[33]

I believe that Native American texts will not only bid for entry into the broad canon of American literature but into the official, institutional canon as well. They will do so, if they do, not only because theoretical developments will prepare us better to understand them, nor simply because pluralists and democrats (I would count myself among them) will urge us to give them a fair shake. If the canon ratifies the present, as I have said, Native American literature cannot enter it until its values achieve or approach social ascendancy; nor can this occur until material conditions insist upon such ascendancy. But our material situation at present is such that the two major premises of Native American literature are already emerging in American culture and demanding attention. The first is that a global, ecosystemic perspective is the necessary condition of human survival and that such a perspective prohibits anthropocentrism. The second is that cultures—whether "advanced" or "primitive"—can sustain themselves without texts but that the absence (or abandonment) of print presents both possibilities and limitations. To the extent that American culture comes to base itself on these two premises will Native American literature establish itself in the canon.

2/

Indian Autobiography:

Origins, Type, and Function

The group of texts I propose to call Indian autobiographies and to treat as a literary genre has been almost entirely ignored by students of American literature—who have, otherwise, been quite interested in the autobiography as literature. This may be because, as already noted, these particular autobiographies were explicitly presented by the whites who wrote them down and published them as historical or ethnographic documents. Perhaps, too, their neglect results from the fact that Indian autobiographies were indeed written by whites, not by the Indians of whose lives they speak; thus, no Indian autobiography, strictly consid-

Nineteenth-century lithograph of Ma-ka-tai-me-she-kia-kiak, or Black Hawk. Courtesy of the Chicago Historical Society, Chicago, Illinois.

ered, conforms to the definition of autobiography "we all know," as James Cox states it, "a narrative of a person's life written by himself."[1]

"Autobiography" as a particular form of self-written life is a European invention of comparatively recent date. Southey is credited with coining the word in English in 1809, and the earliest American book title I have discovered to use it is from 1832. Great labor has recently been expended in the effort to define "autobiography" as a genre. For our purposes, we may note only that the autobiographical project, as we usually understand it, is marked by egocentric individualism, historicism, and writing. These are all present in European and Euramerican culture after the revolutionary last quarter of the eighteenth century. But none has ever characterized the native cultures of the present-day United States.

Although the Indians' sense of personal freedom, worth, and responsibility became legendary, the "autonomy of the [male] individual" was always subordinated to communal and collective requirements.[2] That egocentric individualism associated with the names of Byron or Rousseau, the cultivation of originality and differentness, was never legitimated by native cultures, to which celebration of the hero-as-solitary would have been incomprehensible.

Neither is the post-Napoleonic sense of progressive, linear history at all like the historical sense found among Indian cultures. (A strict account would require noting many variations.) The Sioux have a well-known proverb to the effect that "A people without history is like wind on the buffalo grass." But the understanding of "history" at issue here, if European analogues may be invoked, is more nearly Hellenic than Hebraic. Or, somewhat more precisely, history is not evolutionary, teleological, or progressive. Means for preserving tribal memory were developed in all "culture areas," but these did not privilege the dimensions of causality and uniqueness which mark the modern forms of Euramerican historicism.

Further, while no culture is possible without writing in some very broad sense, no Indian culture developed the phonetic alphabet which Lewis Henry Morgan isolated as the distinctive feature of "civilized" culture. Patterns worked in wampum belts, tattoos, pictographs painted on animal skins or in sand may all be considered forms of "writing." But the black-on-white which distinguishes scription from diction for the Euramerican, the letter and the book, were not found among native cultures in the precontact period. Even later—after John Eliot had transcribed the Bible into a Massachusetts dialect of the Algonquian language in the seventeenth century; after Sequoyah, in the early nineteenth century, had devised a Cherokee syllabary; or the Dakota language, by the late nineteenth century, had become available for inscription—the presence of the grapheme still signified for the Indian the cultural other, the track of the Indo-European snake in the American garden.

Strictly speaking, therefore, Indian autobiography is a contradiction in terms. Indian autobiographies are collaborative efforts, jointly produced by some white who translates, transcribes, compiles, edits, interprets, polishes, and ultimately determines the form of the text in writing, and by an Indian who is its subject and whose life becomes the content of the "autobiography" whose title may bear his name.

I may now state the principle constituting the Indian autobiography as a genre as the principle of *original bicultural composite composition*. I mean thus to distinguish Indian autobiographies from autobiographies by "civilized" or christianized Indians whose texts originate with them and contain, inevitably, a bicultural element, yet are not compositely produced. I mean, as well, to distinguish Indian autobiographies from traditional Native American literature in textual form in which, although there is bicultural composite composition, there is no question of personal origination. Unlike traditional Native literature, the Indian autobiography has no prior model in the collective practice of tribal cultures.

Although there will always be debatable cases (e.g., I would class the many "as-told-to" autobiographies of Indians which have appeared in the twentieth century among autobiographies-by-Indians rather than Indian autobiographies because their subjects' competence in written English allows them to take responsibility for the form of the work to a degree impossible for most Native American subjects of Indian autobiography: but this is, to be sure, a judgment of degree, not kind), it should be possible to demonstrate this particular mode of production for any text claimed for the genre. In this respect, I follow a structural or "syntactic" definition of genre, as in the following formulation of Tzvetan Todorov: "When we examine works of literature from the perspective of genre, we engage in a very particular enterprise: we discover a principle operative in a number of texts, rather than what is specific about each of them."[3] But this turns us back to the issue with which we began: to what extent is it responsible to treat works presented as contributions to history and ethnography as works of literature?

It is surely true that all texts, social-scientific as well as literary, share a narrative dimension, and that no text can evade the orders of language to achieve an innocent or neutral representation of "the order of things." Yet social-scientific and literary texts each have a different epistemological status, the one being bound by the real, the other free of it, at least to the extent it may willfully transform or distort the real. This difference informs the different natures of the scientific and the literary reading as well. The scientific reading is impelled by the desire to foreground the real, to pass as rapidly as possible beyond the orders of the signifier to an engagement with the real-as-signified. (This last, to be sure, is a problematic category: the real need not be taken as transcendental ground but as the ultimate horizon of the text, as history in a specifically Marxian sense, or as the world beyond the text.) The justification for a scientific reading—the condition for cognitive responsibility—typically refers to authorial intention as this is conveyed not so much (or only) through the biography of the author as through his or her text's relation to those discursive rules which define scientific texts.

The decision to read texts discursively marked as scientific in a literary way may also be responsible, however. In such a case we must require the instantiation of sufficient reasons to override the authorial/discursive markings. I would justify a literary reading for Indian autobiographies by reference to the principle of original bicultural composite composition, which constitutes them as a genre of writing. Their particular mode of production means that in Indian autobiographies there is, in Jakobsonian terms, an actual doubling of the sender and of the cultural code which complicates the signifier in precisely historical and demonstrable ways. A literary reading, as I have said, foregrounds not the real-signified but the signifier and the formal signifying practices of the text. Because these practices are determined not only by language but by history, in particular the relations between the general mode of production and the literary mode of production, it should be clear that the scientific and the literary reading differ in no way absolutely but only in their emphases. Given the presence of two persons, two cultures, two modes of production, as well as two languages at work in the formation of the Indian autobiography, it seems reasonable to examine the signifier and the text's signifying practices in some detail, regardless of whether—and how—one may seek passage to the world beyond the text.

The principle of original bicultural composite composition, which provides the key to the Indian autobiography's discursive type, provides as well the key to its discursive function, its purposive dimension as an act of power and will. For to see the Indian autobiography as a ground on which two cultures meet is to see it as the textual equivalent of the frontier. Here, the frontier does not only mean the furthest line of points to which "civilization" has extended itself; rather, to adopt the systemic view of the contemporary ethnohistorian, the frontier also signifies "the reciprocal relationship between two cultures in contact."[4] But, however much it may have been "reciprocal," the "relationship" between Native Americans and Euramericans was never—with the exception, perhaps, of moments during the eighteenth century—one between equals. For the whites, the advance of the frontier always meant domination and ap-

[33]

propriation, and the movement westward was achieved not only with the power of the sword but of the pen as well. To win the continent required not only troops and technology but a discourse of what Foucault would call *assujettissement*, of—in Edward Said's description—"the subjugation of individuals in societies" (or of whole societies) "to some suprapersonal discipline or authority."[5]

During the nineteenth century, part of that discipline was the idea of progressive history as a "scientific" determinism or "law" which authorized the doctrine of cultural evolution, the belief that "civilization" must everywhere replace "savagery." This was the official sanction for the removal of the eastern tribes west of the Mississippi in the 1830s as it was the unofficial sanction for the enormous body of writing about Indians that appeared in these same years. Along with novels, poems, plays, and "histories" of Indians, the decade of Indian Removal saw the production of a new form of writing "by" as well as about Indians, the Indian autobiography. Following native defeat in the Black Hawk War, J. B. Patterson, in 1833, published the first Indian autobiography, the *Life of Ma-Ka-tai-me-she-kia-kiak or Black Hawk*. As Black Hawk had submitted to Euramerican military and political forms, so he now submitted to Euramerican discursive form. But the form of writing offered to this Indian who could not write was not the eighteenth-century "life-and-times" biography; instead, it was the newer form of personal history, the autobiography. Produced as an acknowledgement of Indian defeat, in the ideological service of progressive expansionism, the book made by Patterson and Black Hawk, by admitting an Indian to the ranks of the self-represented, also questioned progressivist expansionism. For the production of an Indian's own statement of his inevitable disappearance required that the Indian be represented as speaking in his own voice. Unlike Indian biographies, Indian autobiographies require contact with living Indians, for it is the central convention of autobiography that the subject speaks for himself. And it is in its presentation of an Indian voice not as vanished and silent, but as still living and able to be heard that the oppositional potential of Indian autobiography resides.

During the first stages of the "invasion of America," the East itself was West, and the towns of the "frontier" were named "Plimoth," Jamestown, and Boston.[6] Contact between the Euramerican invader-settlers and Native Americans led to conflict; the most common "reciprocal relationships" were conquest and captivity, and it should come as no surprise that the first two indigenous forms of history-writing developed in the New World were the Indian War Narrative and the Indian Captivity Narrative.

Recognizing the insatiable colonial appetite for land, Indians—for the most part—chose the "wrong" side in the American Revolution and suffered the consequences of British defeat. By the end of the eighteenth century, the American invasion had pushed forward into the Ohio valley and Daniel Boone's "dark and bloody ground" of "Kentucke" where the by-now traditional frontier relations of battle and bondage were reestablished. Indians fought Americans once more in 1812 and once more lost. After the Treaty of Ghent in 1815, the natives could no longer hope for European support to check the further advance of the new American nation. Jackson's election to the presidency, signaling the rise of the West, signaled also the fall of the red man, for Indian Removal now became a national, not merely a local, priority.

"Indian-haters" avid to appropriate native holdings, and "Indian-lovers" avid to protect the "noble" Red Man from white drink, disease, and depredation joined in supporting the Indian Removal Bill which, after fierce debate in Congress, was passed into law on 28 May 1830. The opposition included Davey Crockett, a western rival of Jackson, and John Quincy Adams, quintessential easterner. For the decade of the 1830s, response to the plight of the Indian was of paramount importance to American thought about history and science.

The forcible removal of the eastern tribes into the "Great American Desert" west of the Mississippi was generally viewed—sadly or gladly—as the inevitable consequence of the advance of civilization. Not white cupidity, but the "scientific law" of cultural evolution, popularly equated with the "doctrine of progress," determined the disappearance of the natives, giving an odor of sanctity to the most violent acts of exploitation and providing the ideological authorization for the wholesale destruction of Native cultures.

Or, rather, for the accession of "nature" to "culture." For, as Roy Harvey Pearce showed some time ago, in nineteenth-century American discourse, Indian "savages" had no "culture." The "customs" of "savagery" could not be dignified as a different form of culture from Euramerican "civilization," nor even a different stage of culture; rather, they were to be seen as the antithesis of culture, its zero degree.[7] In the seventies and eighties after Morgan had defined "savagery" as an evolutionary stage prior to "barbarism" (the category into which most American Indians actually fell), which was itself but a stage prior to "civilization," Friends of the Indian succeeded in their fight to declare the Indian indeed civilizable. But for the 1830s and 1840s, the "savage" remained the one who could never be civilized. As the "Jew" is to the anti-Semite, in Sartre's analysis, or the Oriental to the European in Edward Said's analysis, so was the "savage" to the "civilized" American of the nineteenth century the term for radical alterity, a condition of being which no act could contradict.

Because the Indian "savage" could not himself be "civilized," "civilization" could not help but supplant him. The "aborigines," "Persons of little worth found cumbering the soil," in Ambrose Bierce's unsentimental definition, "soon cease to cumber; they fertilize."[8] As American troops removed Indians to the West in the 1830s, a very considerable interest in this material for fertilizer developed, and a great deal of writing about the "vanishing American" began to appear. New Captivity Narratives, authentic and apocryphal, were rushed to press while older Captivities, along with Indian War Narratives, were reprinted. Cooper's fiction reached the height of its popularity in this period, and gave voice to the typical eastern sadness at the passing of a primitive but noble race. Not sadness but satisfaction was the attitude more usual to the westerner (or southerner), and expressed in the Indian fiction of Robert Bird and William Gilmore Simms, novelists whose knowledge of Indians, unlike Cooper's, was derived not only from the library but from contact as well.

Painters as well as writers became Indian "historians," setting themselves the task of representing Indian life before it was gone forever. George Catlin, still the best known of the Indian-painters, left Pennsylvania for the West in 1830, the year of the Removal Act; his task, he wrote, was to rescue "from oblivion the looks and customs of the vanishing races of native man in America."[9] In every case, as A. D. Coleman has only recently written of the photographer Edward Curtis, a later "historian" of the still-vanishing Indian, all those who took the Indian as their subject sought "to document all aspects of a marvelous culture which was being inexorably destroyed, in such a way as to retain the spirit of the culture and keep it alive."[10] Only the spirit of Indian culture might be kept alive; no intervention in history was believed possible to save it materially from inexorable destruction. And even that spirit would have to be kept alive by those allied to its destroyers: for only they possessed the means of documentation and representation. The Indian himself did not paint things as they "really were"; the Indian could not write. His part was to pose—and disappear.

The West saw the destruction of the Indians not only as inevitable but also as just; but the East, which did not doubt the inevitability of it all, nonetheless questioned its justice. Considering the deeds of their own forebears, ministers in Boston protested Jackson's Indian policy, concerned that the "mistakes of the Puritan founders," their "historical blunders," not be repeated on the "frontier."[11] Urging that we learn from the past, these easterners provided a powerful impetus for the writing of Puritan history. But there was other writing to be undertaken as well, "an act of mere justice to the fame and the memories of many wise, brilliant, brave and generous men—patriots, orators, warriors and statesmen,—who ruled over barbarian communities, and

were indeed themselves barbarians," as B. B. Thatcher explained in the preface to his *Indian Biography* which, along
with Samuel G. Drake's *Indian Biography*, was published
in Boston in 1832. "We owe, and our Fathers owed, too
much to the Indians . . . to deny them the poor restitution
of historical justice at least," Thatcher continued, adding
darkly, "however the issue may have been or may be with
themselves."[12]

The form Thatcher and Drake chose for restitution was
the "life-and-times" form of eighteenth-century biography.
Their Indians are represented as eminent men in the neoclassic mold but they are not yet conceived of as heroes.
Biography writing in the West, on the contrary, was very
much engaged with the heroic and produced not only lives
of that nearly legendary, Indian-like white hero, Daniel
Boone, but, in time, the lives of Indians as well.

In view of Richard Slotkin's influential work on the Boone
material which privileges the explanatory categories of myth
and archetype, it seems important to point out that the
search for an American hero was rooted not only in some
universal human longing, but in some very specific nineteenth-century ideas about history, science, and law[13]. Interest in the *heldensleben* in mid-nineteenth-century America
was spurred by a concern to discover an individual author
of events and to locate historical beginnings—rather than
absolute origins, in Said's useful distinction—in personal
action. We need only think of Carlyle, the contemporary
of these American hero-seekers, to recall how great an explanatory force the belief in "great men" once had. Carlyle's
dictum that history is "the essence of innumerable biographies"—an opinion shared on these shores by Emerson and

Thoreau—is the essence of the nineteenth-century romantic reaction against neoclassic Universal History which, as Louis Mink has written, simply "never made room for . . . the uniqueness, vividness, and intrinsic value of individuals."[14] What is curious to note is that the reaction against Universal History, as Mink further remarks, does not prevent its simultaneous survival in the guise of the doctrine of progress. In this context, autobiography, the self-written narrative of the "hero's" life, will become available both to support this "suprapersonal discipline" yet also potentially to oppose it.

For the decade of Indian Removal was also the decade when a conjunction of historicism and egocentric individualism first brought autobiography as a term and a type of writing to America. In Boston, in the same year Thatcher and Drake issued their Indian biographies, the seventeenth-century "personal narrative" of Thomas Sheperd was published as an "autobiography"; *The Autobiography of Thomas Sheperd, the Celebrated Minister of Cambridge, New England* is the first American book I have found to use the term *autobiography* in its title. The following year, Asa Greene became the first American to apply the term to a "narrative of [his] life written by himself," when he published, in New York, *A Yankee Among the Nullifiers, an Auto-Biography,* under the pseudonym Elnathan Elmwood.

Although Elnathan Elmwood has lapsed into obscurity, we still think of autobiography as a Yankee affair. Those we usually place in the great tradition of personal narrative or autobiography in America—Jonathan Edwards in the colonial period, Benjamin Franklin in the Revolutionary period, Henry Thoreau in the period preceding the Civil

War—are all easterners. So, too, are Henry Adams, the next major figure in this tradition, and, to step into the twentieth century, Gertrude Stein as well. From the first days of settlement until the end of the nineteenth century, the American self tended to locate its peculiar national distinctiveness in relation to a perceived opposition between the European, the "man of culture," and the Indian, the "child of nature." And, for the writers I have named, the European polarity was decisive. The works of eastern autobiography from Edwards through Stein are old-world-oriented and self-consciously literary. (Edwards, Franklin, and Thoreau, however, wrote extensively about Indians.) These autobiographers were conscious of themselves as writers when it was writing that precisely distinguished the European "man of culture" from "nature's child," the Indian—who did not write. The classic eastern autobiographies include scenes of writing (and reading) as important to self-definition. Only with Thoreau, formed in the Jacksonian era of the rise of the West and intense concern with Indians, did the "natural" polarity enter into the autobiographical project. Thoreau's movement from the study to the woods and back was an exemplary journey as fact and as metaphor for Americans of the 1830s and 1840s. (It is interesting, too, to note that pencil-making and surveying were Thoreau's only ordinary sources of income after he stopped keeping school.)

But there is another tradition of autobiography in America for which the Indian polarity was definitive. In this tradition, we have the autobiographies of Daniel Boone, Davey Crockett, Kit Carson, Jim Beckwourth, and Sam Houston. Unlike Yankee autobiography, the western tradition is restless, mobile and, reflecting the split between "high" and "low" culture already hardening in the age of Jackson, explicitly anti-literary. The subjects of western autobiography are all "world-historical" chiefs whose public reputations, like that of Andrew Jackson himself, were first established by Indian-fighting. Yet these men, in comparison to the European or the American easterner, seemed themselves to be "Indians," men of action not letters, hunters and warriors, not preachers or farmers, neither book-keepers nor book-writers. Nearly or wholly illiterate, they rejected the fall into writing and civilization, and balked at cultivating either the field or the page. Defined by Indian War and voluntary or involuntary Indian Captivity, these western autobiographers did not settle down long enough to establish their texts in writing, which, as an act, they largely scorned. Invoking the "natural," oral tradition of the Indian, telling *coup* stories or tall tales, the western autobiographer lived his life apart from writing, going so far as to entrust its actual inscription to another.

Although the "real" Daniel Boone at least once carried a copy of *Gulliver* with him, as the story of the naming of Lulbegrud Creek attests, he was not, himself, interested in writing. If he kept notes for a story of his life, as he was urged, they have not survived. Fairly consistent in signing correspondence "your omble Sarvent," Boone, it would seem, attempted to pass "naturally" from diction to scription.[15] His was exactly the orthographical and grammatological theory Colonel David Crockett espoused in the preface to his autobiography: "I despise this way of spelling contrary to nature. And as for grammar, it's pretty much a thing of nothing at last, after all the fuss that's made about it."[16]

But even Crockett had to acknowledge, as Boone before him had done in collaborating with John Filson, that the book of a man's life cannot be made strictly according to "nature." In Louis Renza's phrase, "Autobiography . . . transforms empirical facts into *arti*-facts."[17] Thus the western autobiographer encountered a problem different from any faced by his eastern counterpart. For, when the eastern autobiographer looked to Europe for a model of the self, he also found a formal model for his book. But, if the western autobiographer, looking to the Indian, found a valuable experiential model, he found no textual model whatever. The solution to this problem turned out to be submission to varying degrees of collaborative composition, where the empirical, natural, and historical "facts" of a man's life were the contribution of the nominal subject of the autobiographical book, while its artifactuality, its grammar, and writing were the contribution of one accredited as the culture-bearer: the journalist-editor or, in Crockett's scornful term, the "critic . . . a sort of vermin," who was, finally, the book's author in the strictly etymological sense (*augere*) of one who augments as well as originates.[18]

Boone's "autobiography," the first of this western line, was written by John Filson, a Pennsylvania schoolmaster saturated in eighteenth-century biographical conventions. Crockett insisted of his "autobiography" that "the whole book is my own, and every sentiment and sentence in it." Yet he "would not be such a fool, or knave either, as to deny that I have had it hastily run over by a friend or so, and that some little alterations have been made in the spelling and grammar." Perhaps the book "is the worse of even that"; still, there is no avoiding "a little correcting of the spelling and the grammar to make them fit for use."[19] To make the book of Kit Carson's life "fit for use" took very nearly an absolute division of compositional labor, for Carson could neither read nor write. Approaching the Indian in incomprehensibility, Carson spoke a language "markedly" different, according to M. M. Quaife, "from ordinary literary English," and expressed his "sentiments" in a "patois" common to mountain men.[20] Sam Houston's autobiography required the mediation of C. E. Lester. When James Beckwourth, born of mixed black and white parentage, who rose to the status of War Chief of the Crow, returned to Euramerican ways and to autobiography, he required the aid of T. D. Bonner to write the book of his life.[21] Thus eastern Indian biography with its orientation to "historical justice" through the textual representation of individual Indian lives provided the motive force for Indian autobiography, while western autobiography with its discovery of composite authorship provided the solution to its formal problem.

After passage of the Indian Removal Act, William Hagan wrote:

> Most of the tribes were prevailed upon to remove by the routine methods of persuasion or bribery or threats, or some combination of these. The three exceptions were a band of confederated Sacs and Foxes, the Creeks, and the Seminoles. Back in 1804 the Sacs and Foxes had signed a treaty under suspicious circumstances at the request of Governor Harrison. It provided for a cession of their lands east of the Mississippi, but did not require removal until the line of settlement reached them. Most of the tribesmen were ignorant of the situation until in the late 1820's peremptory demands were made on them to move. Then a faction led by old war chief Black Hawk, who had opposed

the Americans in the War of 1812 and had subsequently plagued government agents by his conservative policies, denied the validity of the 1804 treaty.[22]

Eventually, in April of 1832, the Black Hawk War broke out, a fifteen-week affair in which large numbers of Illinois militia (among them the young Abraham Lincoln), together with detachments of federal troops, decimated and demoralized Black Hawk's band sufficiently to induce the chief's surrender. Following months of imprisonment at Jefferson Barracks (where Catlin among others came to preserve him on canvas), Black Hawk was brought before his contemporary, the Great War Chief of the whites, "Old Hickory," Andrew Jackson. After their meeting, apparently unaware of the partial coincidence of their routes, the two warriors set out on a tour of the East where both Black Hawk and the president received, to borrow Davey Crockett's phrase, "much custom." Black Hawk was briefly detained at Fortress Monroe and then returned to his people on the Rock River. It was at this time, according to Antoine LeClair, the government interpreter for the Sacs and Foxes, that Black Hawk approached him and did "express a great desire to have a History of his Life written and published."[23]

Although he was highly regarded by both Indians and whites as an interpreter, and reputedly competent in some dozen Native languages, LeClair did not speak English as his own first language. For this (or some other) reason, he engaged the assistance of young J. B. Patterson, editor of the Galena, Illinois, *Galenian*. And it was Patterson, in the role of Black Hawk's editor and amenuensis, who actually wrote the history of Black Hawk's life.

According to LeClair and Patterson, Black Hawk dictated to LeClair who translated his words into English; these were then edited into final form by Patterson. In his 1882 reissue of the *Life*, Patterson wrote, "After we had finished his [Black Hawk's] autobiography the interpreter read it over to him carefully, and explained it thoroughly, so that he might make any needed corrections, by adding to, or taking from the narrations; he did not desire to change it in any material manner."[24] This was a recollection a full half century after the fact, however; but it is all we know of how the manuscript was actually produced. For, as Donald Jackson, Black Hawk's most recent editor, attests, "there are no known documents by which the authenticity of the work can be established."[25]

In a prefatory "Advertisement" from the "Editor," Patterson writes, "It is presumed no apology will be required for presenting to the public, the life of a Hero who has lately taken such high rank among the distinguished individuals of America." The first part of this is entirely conventional and parallels Thatcher's opening statement: "The Author does not propose an elaborate explanation or an apology of any kind, for the benefit of the following work."[26] But the proposal of Black Hawk's as a "Hero's" life goes beyond Thatcher whose Indians, "remarkable characters"— as his title page puts it—though they may have been, are not yet "heroes." Moreover, although they are "individuals who have been distinguished among the North American natives," this is not necessarily to give them "high rank among the distinguished individuals of America" as a whole. Patterson goes beyond Thatcher not only in permitting Black Hawk the context of heroism and national distinction but also in relinquishing his claim to the full authority of the "Author" for the more limited power of editorship. Thus on the title page of each Indian autobiography there appears that fraternal couple so frequently invoked by the American imagination, the White Man and the Indian—Natty Bumppo and Chingachgook, Ishmael and Queequeg, the Lone Ranger and Tonto—but with a difference. For the claim of Indian autobiography is that the white man is silent while the Indian, no longer a mute or monosyllabic figure, speaks for himself.

Patterson's relation to Black Hawk replicates Filson's relation to Boone, and it is indicative of the West's "literary reconciliation to identification with the Indian" that there is extended the graphological supplement, the distinctive property of "civilization," not only to the Indian-like white frontiersman but to Indian "nature" itself.[27] In this way, Black Hawk, no less than the great Boone himself, may speak his life in writing.

The formal similarity of western autobiography and Indian autobiography may be extended to a functional similarity as well—but only to a point. Both, that is, function to affirm the central authority of American progressivist ideology, offering testimony to the inevitable replacement of "savagery" by "civilization." Filson's Boone concludes his "autobiography," saying:

> . . . I now live in peace and safety, enjoying the sweets of liberty, and the bounties of Providence, with my once fellow-sufferers, in this delightful country, which I have seen purchased with a vast expence of blood and treasure, delighting in the prospect of its being, in a short time, one of the most opulent and powerful states on the continent of North-America; which with the love and gratitude of my country-men, I esteem a sufficient reward for all my toil and dangers.[28]

Boone's life and his book are evidence that the long knife and long rifle are adequate to the work of "civilization," driving the "savage" out and transforming the "wilderness" into "one of the most opulent and powerful states on the continent of North-America." Black Hawk concludes his "autobiography" with the assurance that "the white man will always be welcome in our village or camps, as a brother . . . and may the watch-word between Americans and Sacs and Foxes, ever be—'*Friendship*'!" (Jackson, *Black Hawk*, pp. 153–154). But these are not the words of a man basking in success and looking forward to glory; rather, as Black Hawk has announced in the dedication of his book to Brigadier General H. Atkinson, his "conqueror," they are the words of one who is "now an obscure member of a nation, that formerly honored and respected [his] opinions . . . [and one who hopes] you may never experience the humility that the power of the American government has reduced me to." Admitting "the power of the American government," Indian autobiography takes its place beside western autobiography in a discourse of *assujettissement*, the ideological authorization for displacement of the Native.

Whereas victory is the enabling condition of western autobiography, defeat is the enabling condition of Indian autobiography. The narrative of the life of the western hero follows the "emplotment" of American history as the nineteenth century conceived it, and is figured as "comedy," the just progression to a "happy ending" in which the red-skinned "blocking characters" are overcome. "The society emerging at the conclusion of comedy," as Northrop Frye has written, "represents . . . a kind of moral norm, or pragmatically free society."[29] And so it is in *The Autobiography of Daniel Boone*.

Its structure is not only determined by the "facts" of Boone's life, nor even strictly—in Hayden White's terms—by the pregeneric figural preferences of John Filson, but, as well, by the authority and discipline of discourse. The narrative of the life of the Indian "hero" replicates the general ideology of the period formally by structuring that life as a story of decline and fall, or—apparently—as tragedy. (This gives us the curious paradox of *heldensleben* as prisoner-of-war narrative.) For it is only when the Indian subject of an autobiography acknowledges his defeat, when he becomes what Patterson calls a "State-prisoner," that he can appear as a "hero." Even as a "State-prisoner," Patterson writes in his "Advertisement," "in every situation [Black Hawk] is still the Chief of his Band [he has however been superseded by Keokuk], asserting their rights with dignity, fairness, and courage." Perhaps; yet it is only as a "State-prisoner" that he can assert anything at all, or be "allowed to make known to the world the injuries his people have received from the whites." Native American decline is the necessary condition for the comic ascent of Euramerican civilization, and it is by means of this particular structure—the apparent tragedy as actual comedy—that the silent, absent editor speaks his acceptance of progressivist ideology, confirming the inevitability of Indian defeat in the manner of western autobiography.

But Patterson's *Black Hawk* also strongly questions the justice of Indian defeat in the manner of eastern Indian biography. According to Patterson, Black Hawk "thinks justice is not done to himself or nation" in hitherto-published accounts of the War (although Black Hawk could not actually have read them), and part of the motive force behind

the Black Hawk-(LeClair)-Patterson collaboration is the performance of an act of textual "justice." Patterson includes
many instances of the "injuries" done to Black Hawk and
his people, and, speaking in his own voice, he explicitly
criticizes the Treaty of 1804. Patterson also draws back from
full responsibility for anything in the book that may seem
to the "whites" too strong in criticism of their behavior. The
concluding paragraph of his "Advertisement" announces
that "The Editor has written this work according to the
dictation of Black Hawk, through the United States Interpreter, at the Sac and Fox Agency of Rock Island. He does
not, therefore, consider himself responsible for any of the
facts or views, contained in it."

Rather than weakening the oppositional force of the book,
Patterson's disclaimer is, instead, the announcement of its
formal expression. For the *Life* of Black Hawk is not a
biography but an autobiography; if Patterson is not "responsible" for what Black Hawk says, then Black Hawk
himself must be responsible. Here is the unprecedented
instance of an Indian speaking for himself.

Unlike the eastern Indian-biographer, Patterson did not
make his book from the safe distance of Boston or New
York, nor was his subject the "life-and-times" of some by-
gone noble barbarian. Patterson came from Illinois, and he
wrote from Rock Island only a year after the Black Hawk
War. In just five more years, even a western Indian-biographer could echo Thatcher and the ministers of Boston on
the Indians; in a biography of Black Hawk published in
Cincinnati in 1838, Benjamin Drake wrote, "Have we not
more frequently met [the Indians] in bad faith than in a
Christian spirit?" And Drake accepted full responsibility for

his book's purpose "to awaken the public mind to a sense of the wrongs inflicted on the Indians."[30]

I would not minimize the efforts of Samuel Drake, B. B. Thatcher, or Benjamin Drake to do "justice" to the Indian in writing. Yet unlike Patterson, these men adopted the biographical not the autobiographical form which, whatever its author's intentions, cannot help but function in support of the belief that the "savage" has no intelligible voice of his own, that the "civilized" man of letters must speak for him if he is to be heard at all. The Indian biographer, master of books and writing, required no contact with his subject; he had no need to enter into a reciprocal relationship with him. According to Samuel Drake, his *Indian Biography* takes "much of" its material "from manuscripts never before published"; its title page is adorned with a verse from Byron and, interestingly, a verse of Isaiah from what Drake calls the "Indian Bible," no native product but the white man's gift to the red.[31] Appropriately, Drake's book is published by Josiah Drake at the Antiquarian Bookstore, first established in 1830, the year of the Indian Removal Bill. Thatcher, too, is almost entirely indebted to the "archive" for his work, like Drake exploiting the resources of the Antiquarian Bookstore as well as materials from the Harvard Library and other collections.

Turning to books, not to Indians, Drake and Thatcher retained their "exteriority" and kept the full *authority* of the author not as augmentor but as originator. Although the Indian biographer approached the *impensé*, the epistemic unthinkable of the period, when he suggested that Indians "must . . . vanish" only if the constant "wrongs inflicted" on them forced them to vanish, he never went so far as to grant the Indian the right to speak for himself. Whatever injustices and injuries he protested, he was not yet able to protest in the actual form of his work what Gilles DeLeuze has called the indignity of speaking for others. With all his sympathy for the Indian, the Indian biographer still defined him as he would be defined by Robert Frost's murderous Miller, in "The Vanishing Red," as ". . . one who had no right to be heard from."

But it is the central convention of autobiography that its subject speaks for himself. Black Hawk may speak in Patterson's presence, but "The Editor," as we have noted, ". . . does not . . . consider himself responsible . . ." for what is said; in his choice of the autobiographical form, Patterson speaks against progressivist ideology. As discursive equivalent of the frontier, the textual ground on which two cultures meet, the Indian autobiography requires contact between its subject-author and its editor-author. If the relationship is unequal, it is nonetheless genuinely reciprocal. Only by submitting to the Euramerican form of autobiography could Black Hawk speak to the whites at all; only by accepting the graphematic supplement of the editor and the fall into writing and culture could Black Hawk achieve the book of his life, whose final form was not his to determine. Yet an Indian autobiography could be achieved by no white alone. Only by acknowledging reciprocity, abandoning the authority of the author for the more limited authority of editorship, and entering into "contact" with Black Hawk, could Patterson produce the book of an Indian life, a book in which a still-living and formerly unheard voice emerged to speak for itself. This Indian voice—translated, transcribed, edited, polished, interpreted though it was—had never before sounded, not in western autobiography (hostile to it though indebted to it), nor in eastern Indian biography (sympathetic to it but formally indifferent to it).

Patterson's *Life of Black Hawk* was sufficiently popular to justify four more editions the following year in the East and, after many years, an edition published in St. Louis in 1882.[32] For this, the last edition published in Patterson's lifetime, the "editor and sole proprietor" of the *Life*, as he then called himself, provided some revisions of the text, adding material, expanding certain descriptions, and generally elaborating the diction. For these changes, Patterson was alone responsible, Black Hawk having died in 1838. The 1882 edition also received a new title, for the *Life* now became *The Autobiography of Ma-Ka-Tai-Me-She-Kia-Kiak.* Subsequent editions have tended to use the 1882 title, though reprinting the 1833 text as closer to Black Hawk's "own words." Despite this continued interest in Patterson's work, the remaining years of the nineteenth century present no other fully developed instance of Indian autobiography.

3 /

History, Science,

and Geronimo's Story

The first Indian war to be fought after passage of the Indian Removal Act, the Black Hawk War was also the last to be fought east of the Mississippi.[1] Any hope that Indians might live unmolested in the Great American Desert across the river, or even within an Indian state, proved illusory as land-hungry settlers crossed the Mississippi into an area increasingly represented, in William Nash Smith's account, not as a desert but as the "Garden of the World."[2] On the Plains, in the Great Basin and Plateau, in the southwest and the Pacific northwest, the familiar pattern of contact,

S. M. Barrett, Geronimo, and Asa Daklugie at work on Geronimo's autobiography. Photo titled, "How the Book was Made." From the original edition of Geronimo's Story of his Life, *1906.*

conflict, and conquest reasserted itself. Indian war, in William Hagan's bitter phrase, "that great American institution," persisted as the leading edge of history, whose inexorable law decreed that Indians must vanish in the name of civilization.[3] And "progress" created "State-prisoners" and "fertilizer" in abundance.

Through the expansionist 1840s and into the 1850s, the Indian continued to be represented in art and imitated in life. In the East, Henry Wadsworth Longfellow, a Harvard professor and the first to teach *Faust* at an American college, saw Black Hawk in 1837 in Boston, read Henry Schoolcraft's *Algic Researches* (1839), and transformed Schoolcraft's Manabozho into his own Hiawatha. Longfellow's *Song of Hiawatha* (1855) sold out its first printing of 4,000 copies on the day of its publication and completed its first year in print with sales of 38,000. Hiawatha elegiacally counsels his people to abandon the old ways and adapt themselves to the coming of "civilization," but he does so in a verse form which only "civilization" can provide; Longfellow derived *Hiawatha's* trochaic meter from the Finnish epic, *Kalevala*.

In the west, Kit Carson and Jim Beckwourth, following, as it were, the unlettered footsteps of Daniel Boone, turned themselves—temporarily—into white Indians, the better, as Conrad's Kurz would conclude for a later imperialism, to "exterminate the brutes." But by the end of the 1860s, Indians could no longer even serve whites as models in warfare; with the technological advances gained in the Civil War, Indian-like stealth and ecological expertise became largely obsolete in Indian war. The extension of the railroads, the development of sustained winter pursuit (a time when Indians traditionally considered themselves safe from attack), and the perfection of rapid-fire weaponry provided further evidence to confirm the "law" of "history." Not even the fierce resistance of the Plains tribes, it soon became apparent, could impede the triumph of "civilization" over "savagery." Increasingly it seemed that, as General Philip Sheridan supposedly remarked, the only good Indian would be a dead Indian.

There were to be plenty of dead Indians before the "long death" on the Plains was over and the frontier officially closed in 1890. First, however, the Natives would enjoy one famous victory. It was nearly on the eve of America's first Centennial celebrations, on June 25, 1876, that a combined force of Cheyenne and Sioux annihilated General George Armstrong Custer's Seventh Cavalry on the Little Big Horn River. The Custer fight occasioned national interest in its day, and it remains as the Indian fight every American has heard of. Those who know nothing about Indians are still likely to recognize the names of Sitting Bull and Crazy Horse, leaders in the Custer fight. Yet there exists no full-scale contemporary autobiography of these world-historical chiefs nor of other major leaders who fought Custer. This is because the Custer fight was not an Indian defeat; it did not immediately subject these warriors to the military and political discipline of the whites and so it did not either subject them to white discursive discipline.[4]

This is not to say that even the Custer fighters managed to live out their lives as they wished. The march of "civilization" was not to be denied, and they, too, were brought down. White soldiers murdered Crazy Horse before he had uttered more than a few terse remarks to the whites who

---

cared to hear from him. Sitting Bull, after some years spent in Grandmother's Land—Canada—surrendered to the Commander of Fort Buford with the words ". . . I bow my head."[5] Earlier, in 1870, before his submission, Sitting Bull had consented to draw a representation of his coups, and he twice more drew pictographic autobiographies after his surrender. Yet, according to Lynne O'Brien, "In both technique and subject matter, his autobiographies are generally traditional. White influence, shown in such things as his use of paper and pencil, does not interrupt the basic native pictographic design."[6] Even after acknowledging defeat, Sitting Bull "never seriously departed from the traditional rules of pictographic composition."[7] It is O'Brien's conclusion that "his image of himself in his society was not destroyed by defeat. He felt no need to explain his actions to whites in white forms. White armies might defeat him, but white culture could not intrude upon the way he saw himself."[8] Sitting Bull was also murdered by soldiers.

That the Indians were victorious at the Little Big Horn was only an exception to a rule that remained in effect. Through the 1870s and 1880s, Indian war meant Indian defeat and destruction. In 1877, the surrender of the Nez Perces, after their spectacular "flight" (an event that was particularly well covered by the newspapers of the time) focused attention on a defeated Native American who might well have become a hero of Indian autobiography, Young Joseph, or Heinmot Tooyalakekt ("thunder traveling to loftier mountain heights"). But the text, which has been called, at least since 1907, "Chief Joseph's Own Story," is not, as its title seems to suggest, an Indian autobiography; rather, it is a translation by Bishop W. H. Hare of a speech given by Joseph to an audience of congressmen and other government officials, and published in 1879 in the *North American Review* as "An Indian's Views of Indian Affairs," a title more appropriate to its content. Dealing with the usual injustices done to the Indians and describing a war which the *New York Times* for October 15, 1877, called "on our part . . . nothing short of a gigantic blunder and a crime," Joseph's talk gives very little of the story of his own life.[9]

In the 1880s, not only the *New York Times* but most influential easterners spoke out, as their ancestors fifty years earlier had done, against western injustice to the Indians. Yet eastern kindness often was not much better for the Natives than western cruelty. After the work of Lewis Henry Morgan, Indian "savages" could be seen as "barbarians," and so only one step removed from the phonetic alphabet and written "civilization." Now that Indian "savagery" was no longer, strictly, the antithesis of "civilization," it was perhaps possible, as Captain Richard Pratt, founder of the Carlisle Indian School, put it in a famous slogan, to "Kill the Indian and save the man!" It might be said that Pratt's slogan became the rallying cry for the eastern Friends of the Indian as they collectively came to be known. These Friends "put their faith principally in three proposals," as Francis Paul Prucha has written:

> . . . first, to break up the tribal relations and their reservation base and to individualize the Indian on a 160-acre homestead by the allotment of land in severalty; second, to make the Indians citizens and equal with the whites in regard to both the protection and the restraints of law; and third, to provide a universal government school system that would make good Americans [!] out of the rising generation of Indians.[10]

The first step in the destruction of the communal—"communistic," as these Protestant individualists saw it—culture of the Indian was to do away with the collectively held land-base of the tribes. The Dawes Severalty Act of 1887 became the means to this end; as the Indian Removal Act may be taken as the political expression of American thought about the Indian from, roughly, the 1820s through the 1840s, so too may the Dawes Act be taken in regard to the 1880s into the twentieth century. Dawes provided, in William Hagan's account:

> . . . that at his discretion the President could allot reservation lands to the Indians, the title to be held in trust by the United States for twenty-five years. Full citizenship for the Indian would accompany the allotment. Heads of families were to receive 160 acres with similar amounts going to other Indians. The surplus, after the Indians had been taken care of, was to go on the market.[11]

In practice, this introduction to the blessings of private ownership meant pauperizing the Indian. Between 1887 and 1934, when the Indian Reorganization Act instituted a new Indian policy, of the 138,000 acres of land held by the Indians, no more than 48,000 to 55,000 were left to them, and at least half of what remained was desert or semidesert land.

Only a year before passage of the Dawes Act, far from the halls of Congress on the southwestern frontier, Geronimo and his band of some thirty-odd warriors surrendered one last and final time to the twenty-five-hundred-man army of American "civilization" under General Nelson A. Miles.

Not only Geronimo's band of Chiricahua but other, non-offending Apache bands were rounded up and put aboard trains for the malarial conditions of Fort Marion, Florida. Used to the dry heat of the desert, the Apaches in Florida sickened and died with good regularity until, some eight years later, they were shipped northward and westward, now to be prisoners at Fort Sill, Oklahoma.

It was there, in 1904, that Geronimo met Stephen Melvil Barrett, newly appointed superintendent of schools at Lawton, Oklahoma, and affiliated with the University of Oklahoma. Barrett had assisted Geronimo in selling a war bonnet, and shared with him an unfavorable view of Mexicans. In 1905, Barrett asked Geronimo if he would "allow [him] to publish some of the things he had told [him]." Geronimo refused, but, Barrett's account continues, he proposed instead that if Barrett "would pay him, and if the officers in charge [at Fort Sill] did not object, he would tell [him] the whole story of his life."[12] The officers did object, and Barrett wrote to President Theodore Roosevelt, whose interest in Indians was well known, for permission to proceed with Geronimo's autobiography. Barrett's "Introductory" to *Geronimo's Story of His Life*, the book that resulted from their collaboration, prints ten letters of "Endorsements" passing the proposed project up and down the line of command for comment and approval. Before the manuscript was finally published, it would be reviewed by the president and the War Department, whose objections to statements made by Geronimo were duly noted by Barrett. At the president's suggestion, Barrett also "appended notes throughout the book disclaiming responsibility for adverse criticisms of any persons mentioned by Geronimo" (p. xiii). Understandably,

yet I think regrettably, Barrett's "narration of his deal-
ings with the War Department" has been deleted by
Frederick W. Turner in his edition of the Barrett/
Geronimo text, *Geronimo: His Own Story*, the most readily
available modern edition, as "obviously superfluous material."[13] But this obscures the presence of state power at-
tending upon the production of the text, a presence by no
means "superfluous" for our understanding. Turner also
deletes Barrett's "account of Apache/white warfare in the
nineteenth century," and relegates to an appendix an account of Geronimo's surrender.[14] But this, too, deprives the
reader of understanding as it removes the evidence of Barrett's explicit intervention in Geronimo's "own" story, as
well as of Barrett's "own" opinions on these matters.

"Early in October," of 1905, Barrett's "Introductory" continues, "I secured the services of an educated Indian, Asa
Daklugie, son of Whoa [Juh, Who], chief of the Nedni
Apaches, as interpreter, and the work of compiling the book
began" (p. xx). (Whoa had been an ally of Geronimo's in
battle, and he died by drowning, after too much drinking—
as Geronimo would also die, of exposure, following an
alcohol-induced accident.) Exactly how much education
and of what kind Asa Daklugie had is not clear. Geronimo's
manner of narration, according to Barrett, was simply to
tell what he thought important, in the way he thought
appropriate, and then to leave Barrett and his interpreter to
recall and transcribe what he had said. Although Geronimo
would "listen to the reproduction (in Apache) of what had
been told" (p. xxi), answering questions and occasionally
providing further information, it seems inevitable that the
final text (there does not seem to be an original manuscript

extant) is very much the work of Daklugie and, most particularly, Barrett himself.

Like J. B. Patterson, Barrett was no stranger to the frontier;
his father had been a wagon-train boss, and his grandfather
had settled the family in Indian territory in the 1830s. Also
like Patterson, Barrett presented his subject's life in autobiographical form, but there is little else his book has in
common with Patterson's.

Patterson appears to have accepted the task of writing
Black Hawk's *Life* as an opportunity and a responsibility;
neither he nor LeClair who engaged him to the project
conceived of themselves as its initiators. We have already
noted LeClair's presentation of the *Life* as the expression of
Black Hawk's desire, and Patterson, in his "Advertisement"
to the public, affirms and amplifies:

> Several accounts of the late war having been published, in
> which [Black Hawk] thinks justice is not done to himself or
> nation, he determined to make known to the world, the injuries
> his people have received from the whites—the causes which
> brought on the war on the part of his nation, and a general
> history of it throughout the campaign.

Patterson, we recall, presented Black Hawk as "a Hero who
has lately taken such high rank among the distinguished
individuals of America . . . a Warrior, a Patriot and a State-
Prisoner . . . still the Chief of his band, asserting their rights
with dignity, firmness and courage." For Patterson clearly
shared his period's fascination with the *heldensleben* and its
attraction to the new form of autobiography.

But, although in his "Introductory" Barrett acknowledged
that the idea of publishing a life story originated with Ge-

ronimo, in his preface, he gives no indication whatever of Geronimo's active initiation of the project. "The initial idea of the compilation of this work," Barrett writes,

> [is] to give the reading public an authentic record of the private life of the Apache Indians, and to extend to Geronimo as a prisoner of war the courtesy due any captive, *i.e.*, the right to state the causes which impelled him in his opposition to our civilization and laws.
>
> If the Indians' cause has been properly presented, the captives' defense clearly stated, and the general store of information regarding vanishing types increased, I shall be satisfied. (p. v)

Barrett shares with Patterson that reading of history which sees it as the progress of "civilization" and "law" to triumph over "savagery" and "anarchy." And he shares with Patterson the desire to add to the record an Indian's own statement of his people's "defense" and of the "causes" of his personal "opposition" to "civilization." But Patterson's explicit interest in justice and the conflict between nations, an ethical view of historiography, has here become more nearly a concern with fairness and balance, a presumptively neutral, objective, or scientific view. By 1905, the federal government had not treated with the tribes as nations for more than thirty years; the Indian had dropped out of history and could himself determine nothing. For Barrett, Geronimo is certainly no hero. Not only is Geronimo denied the context of heroism, but of individuality as well; for he is no different from "any captive," any "prisoner of war," no world-historical figure, but just another "vanishing type."

What we have, then, is Indian autobiography in the age not of Carlyle but of Hardy; there are no more heroes, and personal agency counts for little. In eastern autobiographical writing, we have moved from Thoreau's bold determination "to brag as lustily as chanticleer in the morning," in a book in which "the I, or first person . . . will be retained,"[15] to Henry Adams's decision to suppress the I, or first-person. Adams was a professional historian whose amateur account of his education was importantly influenced by the new centrality of the mechanical and physical sciences. Barrett, author of *Practical Pedagogy* (1910), was a professional educator, a student of sociology whose amateur attempt at history writing was importantly influenced by the new centrality of the social sciences. For Barrett is interested in the ethnographic record quite as much as the historical record; he permits Geronimo to tell his story as a means to telling the story of the "private life of the Apache Indians"—itself a means to increasing "the general store of information regarding vanishing types." As any-Apache, just another "vanishing type," Geronimo becomes representative of his culture and thus more valuable for the purposes of science than he would be as an extraordinary or distinctive Apache. For we have also moved from the nineteenth century's interest in the determining individual to the twentieth century's interest in the determining culture.

Barrett was a student of "Indian sociology," and his last book, published in 1946 when he was eighty-one, was *Sociology of the American Indians*. He did not use the anthropologists' term *culture* in *Geronimo*—not in his prefatory and introductory remarks, in his notes, nor in paraphrase/translation of any word of Geronimo's. Yet his phrase, "the private life of the Apache Indians," appears consistent with Tylor's 1871 definition of culture as ". . . that complex whole which includes knowledge, belief, art, law, morals, custom, and any other capabilities and habits acquired by man as a member of society."[16] And Barrett's understanding and application of "the culture concept" is generally consistent with its use in American social science of the period by Franz Boas and his students.

"The gospel's course hath hitherto been as that of the sun, from east to west," Richard Sibbes had written in 1630, "and so in God's time may proceed yet further west."[17] Also from east to west had proceeded the new gospel of science in anthropology, borne from Kiel, Germany, to Morningside Heights, New York, by Franz Boas and then carried to far California by Boas's student, A. L. Kroeber, the first to take a doctorate in anthropology under the master at Columbia. Boasian anthropology established itself as a professional, university-based discipline in reaction to the older, amateur American anthropology which went back perhaps to Jefferson and Colden, to Father Heckewelder, Schoolcraft and, most particularly, to the great Lewis Henry Morgan. I shall consider Boas and his influence on Indian autobiography more fully in the next chapter; here, I would indicate three particular areas of disagreement between the new, Boasian anthropology and the older, evolutionary anthropology primarily associated with Morgan. For the explanatory categories of "race" or "natural law," the Boasians substituted the category of "culture." For the "nomological," generalizing, and deductive "comparative method" of the evolutionary anthropologists, they substituted the method called "historical particularism," an "idiographic" approach founded upon a sense of the uniqueness of historical events, and the almost infinitely complex specificity of cultural instances. For ethnocentric rankings of other cultures as "higher" or "lower" as they approached or remained distant from the pinnacle of Euramerican "civilization," they substituted the concept of "cultural relativism," which valorized the "emic" account of cultural phenomena, the view from the "inside," as seen through the eyes of the native informant him or herself—a procedure that required the anthropologist to develop at least some minimal competence in the native language.[18]

Boasian scientific anthropology constituted its field in the mode Hayden White has defined for *fin de siècle* historiography as the mode of irony; sophisticated, self-conscious, skeptical, the new anthropology hypostasized the distinction between "facts" and "interpretations" and set out to gather the former and avoid the latter.[19] Boas's notorious warning against the inference of "laws," even in the sense of generalized probabilities that might govern the field, was a potent factor in the development of American anthropology for nearly half a century.

Barrett, too, appears determined to avoid "interpretation," and to refuse any generalization. Thus he must suppress— as "unscientific" because inevitably "subjective"—ethical categories so far as he can; unlike Patterson, he cannot employ words like *injury, justice,* or *injustice* very readily, neither in his presentation of Apache culture nor in his presentation of the history of Indian-white relations. This is not to say that he is unmindful of the ethical issue; rather, his "ironic" understanding of "objectivity" forces him to affect a "neutral" presentation. In *Geronimo's Story of His Life,* Barrett's chapter 10, for example, "Other Raids" (this is part of the material omitted from Turner's edition), interrupts Geronimo's narrative; here, Barrett speaks in his own voice and gives an account of the equivalent "lawlessness of the frontier" (p. 86) on the part of whites, Mexicans, and Indians. His chapter 18, "Surrender of Geronimo" (Turner prints this separately, as an appendix), concludes:

> We do not wish to express our own opinion, but to ask the reader whether, after having had the testimony of Apaches, soldiers, and civilians, who knew the conditions of surrender, and after having examined carefully the testimony offered, it would be possible to conclude that Geronimo made an unconditional surrender?
>
> Before passing from this subject it would be well also to consider whether our government has treated these prisoners in strict accordance with the terms of the treaty made in Skeleton Cañon. (p. 176)

We infer the editor's unexpressed "opinion" pretty well, but Barrett will not speak the word *injustice* himself. Like Boas, he believes that the "facts" must speak for themselves.

Explicitly, Barrett's only concern is to offer "the reading public an authentic record" of Indian culture and history; and "authenticity"—consistent with "objectivity"—is a function of the "inside" view. Barrett's use of the word *private*, I mean to say, is synonymous with a term like *emic*, or—awkwardly, but perhaps vividly—*actor-oriented*. For "private" does not mean intimate, affective, or individualized but, instead, means from the perspective of the subject. And this seems to be why the autobiographical form was chosen by Barrett—as it would be by Boas's early student, Paul Radin, who as we shall see inaugurated the professional, anthropological variant of the Indian autobiography.[20] Whereas Patterson used the form, consistent with its first appearances in Euramerican culture, as the appropriate vehicle for the extraordinary individual to express his uniqueness, allowing even the Indian who had attained world-historical status to speak for himself, in the twentieth century, beginning with Barrett, the autobiographical form is used to allow the scientist to express his objectivity. The first-person pronoun demonstrates his absence from the text, and so, too, demonstrates the "objective . . . authenticity" of his account.

Ignoring matters of translation, selection, and arrangement in the compilation of the work and, oblivious as yet to both the developed Nietzschean and the developing Heisenbergian problematics in history and science, Barrett, like the professional anthropological Indian autobiographers who came after him, appears to have retained the autobiographical form as an attempt to reject the inevitable "artifactuality" of any textual narrativization of reality. In the ironic mode, neither science nor history has anything to do with ethical choices—or, for that matter, with esthetic ones. Putative questions of justice still force themselves upon one who would only deal in matters of "clear statement" and "proper presentation" but they must be relegated to chapters of their own, to appendices, or footnotes; and the responsibility for interpreting these materials is always the reader's. "Clear statement" and "proper presentation" are also Barrett's sole esthetic criteria. These observations may help us understand the considerable differences in style and structure between Patterson's *Black Hawk* and Barrett's *Geronimo*, as well as the different content of their (nonetheless) similar functions.

Patterson seems to have believed, in Donald Jackson's phrase, that "a noble Indian deserved noble prose";[21] he sustained that belief until 1882 when he issued his final edition of the *Life* as an *Autobiography*, for he not only added some material but elaborated the diction still further. These new words were not Black Hawk's—he had died in 1838—but Patterson's alone. Barrett's any-Indian, on the other hand, appears in a prose that is neutral and flat, an "objective" style, as it were, pretending to a straightforward mirroring of the "order of things," transparently communicating the "facts" of Geronimo's life.[22] The documentary, scientific effect is enhanced by Barrett's use of footnotes; in these, as in parts of the text itself, he quotes others and gives information to balance out the historical and scientific record of "vanishing types" in conflict with "our civilization and laws." Patterson's *Life*, composed in the name of justice, is tragically emplotted; narrated from Black Hawk's point of view, it is a story of decline and fall, terminating in what Frye has called the "epiphany of law." That "law" is nothing but the progressivist vision of the triumph of Euramerican "civilization" over Native American "savagery," and it is part of the discursive function of the work to affirm the "law" of progress. Thus, as I have noted, from the point of view of Patterson and his contemporary readers, the structure of Black Hawk's *Life* is not tragic at all, but comic, the sad comedy of "civilization" progressing to a happy ending in which the red-skinned "blocking characters" are overcome; "the normal response of the audience . . . is 'this should be.'"[23]

But the emplotment of Barrett's *Geronimo* is ironic—from Geronimo's point of view, it would seem, but certainly from Barrett's, for he is the one responsible for the selection and arrangement of the text as we have it. Unlike Black Hawk's *Life*, Geronimo's story, though one of "opposition to our civilization and law," contains no sense of historical *agon*, and itself illustrates no law whatever. A tale merely of things-that-happened, it is structured by the apparently neutral, or natural, categories of time and space. The book is divided into four parts, the first of which ("The Apaches") and the last ("The Old and the New") are largely accounts of Apache culture as a synchronic unity. The diachronic history of particular interest to white civilization is presented in part 3 ("The White Men"), but in its length, detail, and manner of narration this is almost exactly parallel to part 2 ("The Mexicans"): both the second and third parts chronicle successful and unsuccessful Apache campaigns in warfare, and there is no suggestion that the events leading to Geronimo's twenty-year-long incarceration and the effective destruction of Chiricahua culture by the whites are in any way more significant or important than other of Geronimo's fights south of the border. They are not Geronimo's fights, in any case: for none of "The Apaches," "The Mexicans," or "The White Men" is singled out as a world-historical figure, or individualized. Geronimo is no more than an Indian who happened to be present at certain events, not an author of history; even at his Waterloo, he is no Napoleon but more nearly a Fabrizio del Dongo.

It may be suggested that that was how Geronimo saw things and presented them to Barrett. It is not possible effectively to disprove such a view although its consequence is an estimate of Geronimo as quite an obtuse fellow. From the testimony of James Kaywaykla, Samuel Kenoi, and Jason Betzinez, all of whom knew Geronimo, and felt free to find fault with him, whatever else he may have been he was not obtuse or stupid.[24] It seems rather more likely that it is Barrett for whom the events leading up to the final surrender of Geronimo's small band in 1886 have no special importance. Looking back from the vantage point of 1905, and looking through the lens of ironic scientism, Barrett might well have seen them as no different from a long series of Indian defeats, one of the last steps on the road to vanishment.

In his preface, Barrett had announced Geronimo's story in a passive language, establishing it as an expression of white "courtesy" unable to come into existence on its own initiative. He assigns this same passive language to Geronimo in the fourth and last part of the book, even as Geronimo speaks of "Hopes for the Future," and concludes with the specific hope that a further "courtesy," permission for the Apache to return to Arizona, may be granted. For "we can do nothing in this matter ourselves," Barrett's Geronimo says, "we must wait until those in authority choose to act" (*Geronimo's Story of His Life*, p. 216). The "one privilege" Geronimo requested was not granted in his lifetime; he died, as he suspected he might, "in bondage," in 1909. The remnant of his people who wished to go home were allowed to return to the West, to the Mescalero reservation in New Mexico because the citizens of Arizona would not let them in to "their" state.

With tragic reconciliation to the "law of history," Black Hawk had also acknowledged his "humility" before "the power of the American government" (see the dedication), stated his regrets for his former hostility to "civilization,"

[71]

and announced that "the white man will always be welcome in our village or camps, as a brother" (pp. 153–154)—as if there were yet a situation permitting some choice in the matter; as if the Sac and Fox might yet live as a confederated people able to act as well as to suffer. But this is not at all the nature of Geronimo's conclusion. The only action left to him is to tell his story—if the whites permit it; for him to acknowledge defeat would be superfluous. Nor can there be any tragic reconciliation to the newly revealed order of things, for there is neither order nor revelation nor tragedy here: things simply happened as they happened. The history of the Indian in the ironic mode has no particular meaning or pattern; the scienticization of history on this model requires that it be removed from moral judgment as well as from esthetic arrangement. The objective scientist can be neither a moralist nor an artist; he is not responsible for the way things are or for the arrangement of his text; irony is taken as the avoidance of tropes, not as one tropological choice among others. Barrett's account of the "Indians' cause" and the "private life of the Apache" is indeed offered only to stock "the general store of information regarding vanishing types." Thus Barrett's "scientific" contribution—like much of Boas's own, in the view of Leslie White, Marvin Harris, and others—is to provide us with a "factual" increment, the significance of which, although inevitably implied, yet remains to be stated.

In the nineteenth century, historians—whether journalists, painters, poets, novelists, or biographers—had often accompanied or followed immediately after the army to do "justice" to the dispossessed and defeated Indian, at least in their representations if no way else, preserving what the "law" of progress decreed must otherwise vanish. Patterson's *Black Hawk* functioned as part of the Euramerican discourse of *assujettissement*, in confirmation of the progressivist presumption that Indian "savagery" must everywhere accede to white "civilization." Yet it also functioned to question the justice (if not the accuracy) of that presumption, both in the explicit commentary of its editor and its subject and, most particularly, in its very form, in which—and for the first time—the Indian appeared neither vanished nor silent, to speak for himself.

In the twentieth century, it was the imperium of knowledge that advanced against the Indian. The frontier became the field work, Frederick Jackson Turner's key to American history transforming itself into the key to the new, American anthropological science. In the early part of the century especially, it was not so much the individual Indian himself but his culture that would be preserved in the scientist's representations; the Indian autobiography of the historical Hero became the "life history" of the representative type. Yet having rejected the "law" of cultural evolution and its assertion of the supremacy of "civilization," the Boasians had—or at least offered—no explanation of *why* the Indian still had to vanish—a premise they accepted fully, as the urgent injunction to gather and preserve as much as possible as rapidly as possible with no time lost to theorizing, would indicate. The eventual acceptance of the theoretical position of "cultural relativism" seems to have come at the price of its practical inconsequentiality—for a time, at least. Nonetheless, just as Patterson's book both affirmed and opposed that law which justified every depredation against the Indian, Barrett's *Geronimo* extended but also limited what

Fredric Jameson has called the "imperializing hubris of conventional bourgeois science,"[25] whose "objectivity," as Frantz Fanon remarked, is always turned against the native. The new discourse of science sought to establish the claim that none but those whose credentials marked them as bona fide workers in the "knowledge industry"—university-trained and -based professors like Boas and his students or "superintendents of Education" like Barrett—could "objectively" represent the "facts" of a world already divided into the provinces of specialists, anthropologists, and sociologists.

Although, as I have said, the autobiographical form may have been retained primarily as testimony to the "objectivity" and "authenticity" of the scientist's document, the central convention of autobiography, that the subject speaks for himself, does keep the Indian voice alive (however much mediated), as it preserves, though only as information, the Indian culture. In the Dawes period, when Friends of the Indian methodically sought Native destruction not by extermination but by "civilization," this function of Indian autobiography worked against the grain of the dominant social ideology; rather than try to kill the Indian and save the man, Indian autobiography presented the man inseparable from his Indian-ness.

4 /

The Case of

Crashing Thunder

As Barrett moved out of the classroom for his exercise in Indian autobiography with Geronimo, American anthropology, which already had a substantial presence in the field, was increasingly moving into the classroom. I refer to the event I have already remarked, the arrival of Franz Boas at Columbia in 1896. After the turn of the century, American anthropologists would no longer be largely self-taught, sponsored by the government or the great urban museums; rather, they would be university-trained, -accredited, and -affiliated.

Boas was clearly an extraordinary figure, not only a teacher

Sam Blowsnake (Crashing Thunder) about 1902. Courtesy of the Jackson County Historical Society, Black River Falls, Wisconsin.

but a *maître* in the grand sense, whose students often became disciples and, in several cases (Kroeber, Mead, Sapir, Radin, Benedict) virtual masters themselves. Boas published extensively—a "five-foot shelf" of studies on Native linguistics and philology, on folklore, art, and literature and, most particularly, on ethnography. The Kwakiutl were, as anthropologists say, "his people," and it is impossible even today, some forty years after his death, to refer to the Kwakiutl without referring to Boas's work. Yet he did not—like his contemporaries Sigmund Freud and Ferdinand de Saussure—found what Foucault calls a field of discursivity, a written discourse which itself gives rise to the endless possibility of further discourse, or a discipline, like psychoanalysis or structural linguistics. Boas's contribution to American anthropology—the qualifier is necessary and points to a limit—is indisputable, and this is so regardless of whether there is or ever was a Boasian school as such; regardless of whether his influence achieved the seminal overture to rigor and scienticity his admirers claim, or only instead the installation of a constricting orthodoxy as his most severe critics would have it.[1]

Boas seems to have accepted the image projected by *fin de siècle* imperial capitalism of the world as constituted by forces in competitive opposition and to have founded his science upon it. This binary vision, what Jack Goody has termed the "Grand Dichotomy," exists, certainly, today and has roots traceable to the Greeks and the Hebrews.[2] Yet it had particular effectivity as an explanatory paradigm at the end of the nineteenth century, when—to offer only a partial sampling—it structured Mallarmé's or Henry James's sense of the opposition (not merely the difference) between life and art; de Saussure's extension of the classic bourgeois opposition between the individual and society to language in the opposition of *langue* and *parole*; and Freud's imperial psychomachia between the id and the superego (resulting, if all goes well, in the colonization of the id's territory by the ego). All Europe, as Edward Said's *Orientalism* has shown, divided the world into the Occident and the Orient, the domain of the rational, white, civilized "us" and the mindless, dark, savage "them." And it is no wonder, in this context, that Nietzsche determined an attack on the very concept of logical opposition itself as a major task for philosophy.

For Boas, the central opposition was that presumed to exist between fact and theory or interpretation. In this, he was responding to the excesses of his nineteenth-century predecessors who had tended to reason deductively from broad generalizations of a comparative and evolutionist nature. The "laws" they discovered by this method, as Boas easily demonstrated, were based on very little solid, empirical evidence. But Boas was sceptical not only of laws achieved by deduction, but of general theories of phenomenal lawfulness of any kind in the social sciences. In 1936, he wrote:

> In my opinion a system of social anthropology and "laws" of cultural development as rigid as those of physics are supposed to be are unattainable in the present stage of our knowledge, and more important than this: on account of the uniqueness of cultural phenomena and their complexity nothing will ever be found that deserves the name of a law excepting those psychological, biologically determined characteristics which are common to all cultures and appear in a multitude of forms according to the particular culture in which they manifest themselves.[3]

[77]

Marvin Harris, who quotes this passage as an instance of "Stacking the Cards Against the Nomothetic Mode," comments perceptively on Boas's "supposed to be" in relation to the laws of physics, and concludes, "one inevitably becomes impressed by the amount of effort lavished in proving that chaos was the most salient feature of the sociocultural realm."[4] To the extent that this was so, we may remark the degree to which Boas's scepticism in regard to social scientific law, along with his insistence on the study of independent and "unique" particularities whose interrelation *cannot yet* be stated mirrors the dominant social ideology of the period. Like American atomistic social thought of the early twentieth century, Boasian anthropology emphasized the disparities and differences, the gaps and fissures of the field, rather than its regularities, its discoverable principles of coherence. To publish pages of blueberry pie recipes in Kwakiutl, as Boas did, with no particular indication of their significance is to practice science in the ironic mode.

The critique of laws arose out of a critique of theory; it was the comparative evolutionists' adherence to a priori theory that led to the wild errors of their deductionism. If this aspect of Boas's attack on the evolutionists, as I believe with Marvin Harris, Leslie White, and others, was unfortunate, it nonetheless had a positive side to it. For Boas's critique of comparative evolutionism was also a critique of ethnocentrism. Nineteenth-century anthropologists like Tylor and Morgan, recall, not only described differing degrees of cultural complexity but judged differing degrees of cultural advancement. For them, Western "civilization" was the pinnacle of progress; other cultures could be judged "higher" or "lower"—more or less "primitive"—as they stood nearer or further away from the Western standard. Boas's insistence on a perspective of cultural relativism, his demonstration that there was no noncultural measure by which cultures could be evaluated, had enormous importance in a period when Friends of the Indian were militantly engaged in americanizing him for his own good. There is a good deal of evidence that Boas and his students were as convinced as Daniel Boone of the superiority of Western values; yet their insistence on a relativist research strategy had more than merely academic consequences, and it was with good reason that the americanizers took the anthropologists as their enemy.

Yet, just as it might have been possible to recommend inductionism without attacking the legitimacy—indeed, the inevitability—of interpretation, theory, and general laws, so, too, might it have been possible to criticize the ethnocentric bias of the observer differently from the way Boas did. Locked in, as it were, to the "Grand Dichotomy," Boas seems to have determined that the best corrective to observer bias was to privilege the bias of the observed, the "emic," or inside, view. As Harris puts it, ". . . the definitive test of a good ethnography was whether or not it faithfully mirrored the world of the natives *as the natives saw it*."[5] Thus, "Boasian fieldworkers . . . saw their primary mission to be that of finding out how natives think."[6] In this aim, they trapped themselves, as it were, between two "emics," for they were forced to choose between their own or their informants' cultural perspective. As a result, they tended not to search for "etic" criteria, to define standards compatible with a panhuman scientific epistemology.

One concerned "to find out how natives think" is likely to find the autobiographical method attractive. For, as Paul Radin put it in what became for him a characteristic ex-

planation, the purpose of Indian autobiography was to "throw
. . . light upon the workings of an Indian's brain," to provide
an "inside view of the Indian's emotional life" in a document
richer than those "ethnological memoirs . . . that . . . represented but the skeleton and bones of the culture they
sought to portray."[7] Yet Boas himself never quite accepted
the scientific usefulness of the autobiographical method in
anthropology. In one of the last pieces he prepared for publication, he even went so far as to speak of Indian autobiographies as "of limited value for the particular purpose for
which they are being collected. They are valuable rather as
useful material for a study of the perversion of truth brought
about by the play of memory with the past. The rest is not
much more than an account of customs collected in the
usual way."[8] Earlier in his life, Boas may well have felt less
strongly about the autobiographical method, so that his
dedicated student, Paul Radin, as he collected autobiographical narratives, might believe himself to be working
in a way entirely consistent with Boas's aims.

At Boas's suggestion, Radin did field work among the
Winnebago from 1908 to 1913, the year in which he published his first attempt at Indian autobiography, the "Personal Reminiscences of a Winnebago Indian." This brief
narrative of the Winnebago Warudjáxega, whose name is
translated as "terrible thundercrash," appeared in the *Journal of American Folklore*, edited by Boas. Consistent with
Boas's emphasis on the importance of Native languages for
scientific work, Radin printed the Winnebago text, as his
informant had written it, below the English translation,
warning, however, that "the English rendering is liable to

an interpretation . . . which may be utterly unjustified by the Winnebago itself" (Radin, *PR*, p. 294). Although he could not "very well advocate the learning of Winnebago as an essential preliminary to the interpretation of the above pages . . ." still, Radin asserted, "that is, of course, what must be demanded of all those who refuse to accept approximations" (*PR*, p. 294). After this first Indian autobiography, however, Radin would never again publish the original texts of his informants nor emphasize the "approximate" nature of his own English versions.

I have already quoted Radin concerning his intention, with this initial and particularly rigorous Indian autobiography, to illuminate the Native heart and mind; his would also be a document richer than those "ethnological memoirs . . . that . . . represented but the skeleton and bones of the culture they sought to portray . . ." (*PR*, p. 293). "The answer to the 'dry-as-bones memoirs,'" Radin explained, has been to have them interpreted, either (it would seem) by a professional or amateur non-Native anthropologist, or by a "civilized" Indian who would then render old memories "in poetic English" (*PR*, p. 293). Radin's more scientific solution is to eschew all interpretation and to choose as informant "a real Indian and not a Christian looking back upon a 'romantic' past" (*PR*, p. 293).

The "real Indian" and the "romantic" Indian: for Paul Radin early in the twentieth century it was as if the two stood in opposition to each other, demanding that the interested observer choose between them, and by that choice define him or herself as either a scientist or an artist, the first readily able to convey the "real" with accuracy but liable to do so in a sterile, skeletal fashion; the second readily able to convey the flesh-and-blood vitality of an Indian's life, but liable to sacrifice accuracy and exactitude. Although the powers of art fascinated Radin all his life long, his own chosen way of knowing was the way of science; how to be scientific with lively feeling became the central problem of Radin's experiments with Indian autobiography.

Radin's "real Indian" informant for the "Personal Reminiscences" was "one of those serious and sedate middle-aged individuals whom one is likely to meet in almost every civilization . . ." (*PR*, p. 293). To say this, of course, is already to offer an interpretation, to bias the reader's view of the account which is to follow. But this does not seem to occur or to matter to Radin here. Radin's informant, Warudjáxega, was certainly not an Indian nostalgic for a "romantic," aboriginal past; on the contrary—he was a recent convert to the peyote religion and committed to the view that the old Winnebago ways were pernicious and false. Radin's fourth footnote reminds the reader that "It must be remembered that the narrator was no longer a pagan [!?] when he dictated these texts, and the old beliefs seemed false to him" (*PR*, p. 303). But it does not either occur or matter to Radin, at this point, that such a distinctly anti-romantic view of traditional Winnebago lifeways might in itself constitute a distorting lens that could separate the scientist and his audience from an accurate "inside view" of the "real Indian" and of "the culture to which he belonged" (*PR*, p. 293).

It was also in 1913 that Radin completed a rather different sort of ethnographic work from Indian autobiography. His monumental *The Winnebago Tribe* was the paper accompanying the Thirty-Seventh Annual Report of the Bureau of American Ethnology for 1915–1916 (it was not actually published until 1923). This was a comprehensive survey of Winnebago history, social and ceremonial organization, and the like. But *The Winnebago Tribe* also contained a number of first-person narratives of various lengths obtained from several Winnebago informants, two of whom were identified as "J. B." and "S. B." "J. B." was Jasper Blowsnake, or Warudjáxega, the subject of the 1913 "Personal Reminiscences"; "S. B." was Jasper's younger brother, Sam Blowsnake, also known as Big Winnebago, whose birth-order name was Hagaga. Sam, not Jasper, the "real" Crashing Thunder, would become the subject of *Crashing Thunder: the Autobiography of an American Indian*. In reference, it would seem, to these first-person narratives, Radin wrote in his preface that "Throughout the work, the Indian has been allowed to tell the facts in his own way."[9] For "It has been the aim of the author to separate as definitely as possible his own comments from the data obtained . . ." (*WT*, p. 47). It was precisely upon such a "separation," indeed, that Radin's conception of the scienticity of his autobiographical work depended. For Radin shared Boas's hypostasization of the distinction between fact and interpretive theory, between the objective and the subjective presentation: to be "objective" was to choose the *Native's* subjectivity, to show the world as he saw it.

In 1920, Radin published a second Indian autobiography, "The Autobiography of a Winnebago Indian." This was the story of Sam Blowsnake, identified in the text as S. B.; it is this text on which *Crashing Thunder* would be based. Like the "Personal Reminiscences," the "Autobiography" appeared under scientific auspices and in the Boasian milieu in the *University of California Publications in Archeology and Ethnology* edited by Alfred Kroeber, the first to take a doctorate in anthropology with Boas at Columbia. In a brief introduction, Radin further considers some of the issues he had raised in 1913. This time it is not so much the distortions of "romance" that concern him but, rather, the sterility that may result from too much "sophistication" and "theory." These, like romantic poeticizing, are conceived as likely to prevent the scientist from directly presenting the "real Indian." Using very nearly the same words as he had in 1913, Radin claimed that this present autobiographical text was "likely to throw more light on the workings of the mind and emotions of primitive man than any amount of speculation from a sophisticated ethnologist or ethnological theorist."[10] Again the attraction of the autobiographical method lies in its ability to supply that "atmosphere" (A, p. 1) apparently lacking in most ethnological description. While it is true that "atmosphere" seems more nearly a quality of artistic than of scientific discourse, it would not be correct to claim that Radin has shifted his ground. For he claimed not to have sought out "some definite personage," the kind of highly individuated character a novelist might present but, once again, a "representative middle-aged individual of moderate ability" who could "describe his life in relation to the social group in which he had grown up" (A, p. 2).

Before reworking "The Autobiography" for *Crashing Thunder*, Radin once ventured outside the confines of science into what was ostensibly fiction. In 1922, he prepared a chapter called "Thunder-Cloud, a Winnebago Shaman, Relates and Prays" for Elsie Clews Parsons's *American Indian Life*. Parsons, also a student of Boas (who contributed to the book; A. L. Kroeber wrote the introduction), wanted to broaden the appeal of anthropological material concern-

ing the Indian beyond the community of professional researchers but still to retain the accuracy of science. Her way
to avoid romance, what she called merely bringing "Fenimore Cooper up to date," was to have prominent anthropologists write fictional accounts of aspects of the cultures
they had studied.[11] Most of these took the form of biographical or autobiographical narratives. Despite what Kroeber
called the "fictional form of presentation devised by the
editor,"[12] Radin's "Thunder-Cloud," along with other of the
characters in Parsons's book, was real enough.[13] Thunder-
Cloud had made an extensive appearance in the 1913 "Personal Reminiscences," he had told of his fasting experiences
in *The Winnebago Tribe*, and he had received mention in
"The Autobiography." The monologue ascribed to him in
Parsons's book is hardly a work of fiction; rather, it is a
composite of two first-person narratives Radin had recorded
for *The Winnebago Tribe*—"Thundercloud's fasting experience" and "How an Indian Shaman cures his patients."
The "fictional" Thunder-Cloud, like the unnamed shaman
whose narrative is assigned to him in Parsons's book, is said
to be living his second life on earth—as opposed to the
"real" Thunder-Cloud living his third life. Otherwise, except for an elaboration of the diction to produce a "poetic
English" (*PR*, p. 293), Radin's fiction writing exactly re-
produces his scientific writing.

Finally, in 1926, Radin published *Crashing Thunder: The
Autobiography of an American Indian*. This is, as I have
said, the life history not of Jasper Blowsnake, Warudjáxega,
"terrible thunder-crash," or the real Crashing Thunder, but
of his younger brother, Sam. In his introduction to Sam's
1920 "Autobiography," Radin had told his readers he had
made no attempt to influence his informant "in the selection

of the particular facts of his life which he chose to present," and that "So far as could be ascertained the Indian wrote the autobiography in two consecutive sessions in a syllabary now commonly used among the Winnebago" (A, p. 2). Radin did not, however, publish the original as he had in 1913, but only his own translation, made "on the basis of a rendition from his interpreter, Mr. Oliver Lamere, of Winnebago, Nebraska" (A, p. 2). In the preface to *Crashing Thunder*, Radin gives a somewhat fuller account of "Crashing Thunder's" production of the autobiography, one which, in its acknowledgment of Radin's persistence in overcoming "Crashing Thunder's" reluctance to write his life (see the preface, p. x), complicates his claims to noninfluence. Radin's account in *The Road of Life and Death* of how he obtained the Winnebago Medicine Rite from Jasper Blowsnake, and his curious encounter (in 1958) with Mountain Wolf Woman, sister of Sam and Jasper Blowsnake, suggest that this most learned and urbane scientist could be relatively unsophisticated in his understanding of what might constitute influence upon an informant.[14] Although it may be inevitable, one must agree with Nancy Lurie that surely "an element of coercion was involved with . . . Crashing Thunder" (Lurie, *MWW*, p. 93). But apart from the indirect influence Radin (like any other anthropologist) may have exerted upon his informants, there is the direct influence he surely exerted upon the final text of their autobiographies.

Although it is based on the 1920 "Autobiography," *Crashing Thunder* is very different from it. The 92 pages of "The Autobiography" have been expanded to 203 pages by the addition, as Radin says, of "Certain things . . . that Crashing Thunder had told me on previous occasions."[15] Part 2 of "The Autobiography," called by Radin "My Father's

Teachings," appears in *Crashing Thunder* not as a separate section, but variously distributed throughout the narrative; instead of the 351 footnotes Radin provided for "The Autobiography," there are only 32 footnotes in *Crashing Thunder*. In "The Autobiography" a great number of words appeared in parentheses. Radin had initiated this practice in the "Personal Reminiscences," where, he had explained, the parenthetical words were his own additions to the text to "complete the sense" (Radin, *PR*, p. 294). There are no parenthetical words in *Crashing Thunder*, however, and, although this does free up the movement of the narrative, it also tends to obscure the editor's participation in the production of the text.

The changes I have noted between "The Autobiography" and *Crashing Thunder* are all the result of Radin's working of the Indian's words. Even if we grant that both "The Autobiography" and *Crashing Thunder* present the facts as told by an Indian, with no intentional attempt on the part of the anthropologist to influence him (this would be to grant a lot, perhaps too much), we would still have to remark that the same "facts" appear in very different forms. But this is only to remind ourselves that ethnographies, like histories (as well as fictional narratives) are texts, and that no text can innocently represent the "order of things" independently of the orders of language. Radin's selection from and arrangement of the available materials, his decisions in matters of translation—indeed, every aspect of its mode of presentation—make *Crashing Thunder* an interpretation of a life, one that is, in its turn, in need of interpretation.

For example, in reworking "The Autobiography" for *Crashing Thunder*, Radin revised his earlier translation, ostensibly in the interest of achieving greater accuracy and authenticity. He may well have achieved this aim; yet some of his retranslations seem more nearly artistically than scientifically effective. I will let one instance stand for many. The second paragraph of "The Autobiography" reads:

> I was a good-tempered boy, it is said. At boyhood my father told me to fast and I obeyed. In the winter every morning I would crush charcoal and blacken my face with it. I would arise very early and do it. As soon as the sun rose I would go outside and sit looking at the sun and I would cry to the spirits. (A, p. 3)

Here is how this passage appears in *Crashing Thunder:*

> I have been told that I was a good-tempered child.
> During childhood my father told me to fast and I obeyed him. Throughout the winter, every morning, I would get up very early, crush charcoal, and then blacken my face with it. As soon as the sun rose would I go outside and there gazing steadily at the sun, make my prayer to the spirits, crying. (CT, p. 1)

Syntax and diction have been modified in accord with, if not Victorian, at least pre-modernist concepts of stylistic elegance. The rhythm has been changed; the parataxis of the first has, in general, yielded to a more nearly hypertactic style in the second. In particular, the inversion ("would I" for "I would"), the substitution of the more meditative-reverent "gazing" for the neutral "looking," the addition of the descriptive "steadily," and the rising inflection of the participial terminative, all seem strong markers of a literary motivation. Another change in the direction, as it would

[88]

initially appear, of greater literariness may, however, be more nearly intended to increase the scienticity; that is, the ostensible objectivity of *Crashing Thunder*. In 1920, Radin translated S. B.'s concluding remarks as, "This is the work that was assigned to me. This is the end of it" (A, p. 67). But in 1926, we have, "This is the work predestined for me to do. This is the end of it" (*CT*, p. 203). Here is a change introduced, it would seem, both for its dramatic effect and for its support of Radin's scientific stance of nondirective objectivity. In any case, the issue of literalness and literariness in translation is everywhere important in *Crashing Thunder*, as it is in the life history generally.[16]

This is not, however, to legitimize the debate over whether *Crashing Thunder* is more nearly a work of science or of art, a debate which has mistakenly persisted to the present day. In 1961, Ruth Underhill, a fine ethnologist and collector of Indian autobiography, wrote that in *Crashing Thunder* ". . . Radin was artist rather than ethnologist."[17] A different opinion was expressed by L. L. Langness in a broad survey of the life-history field in anthropology. Langness, in 1965, pronounced *Crashing Thunder*, in effect, a masterpiece of early science, "The beginning of truly rigorous work in the field of biography [*sic*] by professional anthropologists." Langness repeated this estimate in 1981.[18]

Such a debate mistakes the nature of narrative in general and of Indian autobiography in particular. For it is of the nature of narrative always to be a textualization of the facts, never the facts themselves. And the material and historical mode of production of the text weights the particular selection from and arrangement of all the available facts, as the discursive rules marking the literary from the scientific text urge choices of language which may appear more literal or more literary to a given reader. It is the reader, finally, as I have claimed earlier, who must responsibly decide whether to read through the text and pass as rapidly as possible to the world beyond, or to foreground the signifier, for a protracted time and remain within the textual system of signification. The bicultural composite that Indian autobiography is makes it, in particular, as literary *or* as scientific text, an expression not only of its subject's life and culture but of its editor's life and culture as well: as Dick Cushman and George Marcus have recognized recently for "ethnographies as texts," that ". . . rhetorical analysis is prior to an evaluation of truth claims."[19] I have argued for the literary reading of Indian autobiographies; but the "priority" of "rhetorical analysis" even for scientific readings specifically concerned with the evaluation of "truth claims" must be acknowledged.

Yet, in his preface and introduction to *Crashing Thunder*, Radin reaffirmed his sense of the opposition between the "real Indian" known to the scientific professional and the Indian of "romance" more familiar to the "common man." Radin is sympathetic to the scepticism of the "commonsense man, the man in the street," toward the "academically trained scholar" who never seems to capture "what the real Indian is like" (Radin, *CT*, p. xv). This scepticism results from some by now familiar demons, from the scholar's dry reliance on "the usual external fashion which is the pride of scientific procedure among ethnologists" (*CT*, p. x), and from the delusion of the man in the street by—Radin here calls the standard roll of romantic mystifiers—Rousseau, Chateaubriand, and Cooper. But now Radin wants not only to assert the epistemological superiority of his objective science-of-the-inside-view to "romance" in its capacity to present the "real" but, as it were, explicitly to challenge romance on its own ground. There "is, in fact, infinitely more romance," Radin asserts, "—if it is romance we are seeking and most of us are—in trying to obtain an approximately accurate account of what this Indian of our childhood imagination actually is, how he thinks, feels, reacts, adapts himself to the varying conditions of life, than in rehearsing all the scenes of Chateaubriand and Cooper" (*CT*, p. viii). It is hard to know exactly what Radin meant by this. On the one hand, he seems to be offering the simple observation that truth is stranger—more romantic—than fiction. On the other hand, he may be claiming that the pleasure of genuine intellectual mastery through understanding is superior to the pleasure of fantasied mastery through daydreaming. Thus, instead of the "romance" of the "childhood imagination," the particular achievement of the nineteenth century and of art, Radin proposes the adult romance of the real and actual, the special promise of twentieth-century science.

Just as Radin probably influenced his informants, and as he certainly influenced the final text of their accounts, so, too, in *Crashing Thunder* did he seek to influence his audience—in spite of his claim that any such influence is pernicious—and, moreover, to influence them this time with literary references—in spite of his insistence that he was doing objective science. For if Cooper and Chateaubriand have stood in the way of our perception of the real Indian, so must the analogues Radin himself proposes stand between us and the facts. In reference to "Crashing Thunder's" "honesty" as a narrator, Radin writes, "Herein lies the fundamental value of this document for all those who are interested in the *comédie humaine*" (*CT*, p. xxi), with an allusion (at least) to Balzac, and with a proposal, which I shall soon describe, for a structural model of the text. In 1913 and 1920, the Indian autobiography's search for the real Indian turned up a "serious and sedate" (*PR*, p. 293), "representative middle-aged individual," but no "definite personage" (A, p. 2). But in 1926, the "real" and "representative" Indian of the scientist has become someone whose "adventures and tribulations . . . seemed to bear all the earmarks of a true rake's progress" (*CT*, p. x). If Radin in *Crashing Thunder* has succeeded in his scientific project of giving us a real Indian, he certainly cannot have given us a representative Indian—unless the typical Winnebago is to be viewed as a "rake." But it is only Radin's "outside influence" that encourages us in this view of "Crashing Thunder."

So great a "rake" is "Crashing Thunder" that "Benvenuto Cellini's life was drab in comparison," Radin proclaims (*CT*, p. xviii). We are also to think of Jung as we read, for it is asserted that "Crashing Thunder" can interpret "dreams in the most approved [?] Jungian fashion." And there is Voltaire, for "Crashing Thunder" "ends his account fittingly [?] and in the most approved proved [?] style of Voltaire. He, too, like Candide, was going to settle down. He was happy and his wife had a new baby" (*CT*, p. xxiv).

Here Radin clearly indicates his sense of the structure of *Crashing Thunder* which is not, as Ruth Underhill thought, that of a religious confession, of a "drama, centering around [*sic*] a religious experience."[20] Although, as David Brumble has observed, the particularly Christian form of confession might well have been known to "Crashing Thunder" and

thus should not be seen as Radin's imposition on the material, this "romantic" vision does not operate to structure
the text as we have it.[21] Rather, it is the comic emplotment
that we find—just as we do in *Candide*. For the "progress"
of the "rake" or the naif to reform or reconciliation, embed-
ding himself in the social matrix, is a comic progress, whether
it leads to Candide's garden or to a rise from the analyst's
couch and an "adjusted" return to the world. The case of
religious confession is different precisely because of its socially transcendent nature. Religion, decidedly, is of great
importance in *Crashing Thunder*, but its importance lies
more nearly in its ability to teach us how to achieve a decent
life in this world—what "Crashing Thunder" calls "getting
along nicely"—than in its ability to teach us the subordinate
status of this world to some other. *Crashing Thunder* follows
the educational ascendant of comedy to a happy ending.
"Before I joined the peyote," the narrator says in the "Finale," "I went about in a most pitiable condition, and now
I am living happily and my wife has a fine baby" (*CT*,
p. 203). His personal happiness is also explicitly social, for
". . . I go about everywhere telling everyone that this religion is good," and "Many, likewise, have joined this religion and are getting along nicely" (*CT*, p. 202).

To "get along nicely" in this new manner depends on
giving up the traditional Winnebago ways. For, "Crashing
Thunder" tells us, "It is false this giving of pagan feasts, of
holding the old Winnebago things holy, such as the medicine dance and all the other customs" (*CT*, p. 202). "Crashing Thunder" is certainly "not a Christian looking back upon
a 'romantic' past," but is it only his antiromantic perspective
on the old ways that makes him more nearly "a real Indian"

(*PR*, p. 293) than those somehow-not-so "real" Indians Radin warned against in 1913? For Radin's "real Indian" of science, whose account nonetheless provides more romance even than romance itself, is certainly a Christian too, though one who tells a very different story about the loss of the old ways from those told by the nineteenth-century world-historical chiefs. For the warriors, the decline and fall of their traditional culture and the submission to new ways could not be seen comedically as "living happily" or "getting along nicely." Certainly Black Elk, as we shall soon see, a man who knew of the peyote church and valued religion at least as deeply as "Crashing Thunder," could not see the comedy of civilization as anything but tragedy.

This far I have followed Radin's work in Indian autobiography to its culmination in *Crashing Thunder* in such a way as to show how, in practice, the theoretical prescription to keep fact and interpretation separate could not be followed. This, I have argued, was the case in spite of Radin's efforts to sustain the distinction. In what follows, I want to examine some other aspects of his practice which bear, to be sure, on the literariness or scienticity of his autobiographical texts, but also on his status as rigorous (Boasian) scientist; that is, as one for whom method, not temperament, inclination, or ingenuity, ruled. I do not know the degree to which Radin's contemporaries in the field may have attributed, as Radin did, the same materials to different informants, confused materials, and—intentionally or accidentally—misrepresented the nature of their influence on, and alteration of, materials. My suspicion is that Radin—a dedicated and highly sophisticated researcher—was not, in these regards, very different from his

peers. If this were indeed the case, it would have a bearing
on our understanding of the history of anthropology in the
first three decades of the twentieth century, a period when
it was rigorous method, precisely, that constituted the claim
to scientific authority among Boasian anthropologists.

Radin's publications in the field of Indian autobiography
extend from 1913 to 1945, and include: Jasper Blowsnake's
"Personal Reminiscences of a Winnebago Indian" (1913);
Sam Blowsnake's "The Autobiography of a Winnebago Indian" (1920); Thunder-Cloud's monologue in Parsons's
"Thunder-Cloud, a Winnebago Shaman, Relates and Prays"
(1922); the many autobiographical narratives in *The Winnebago Tribe* (1913, 1923); the expansion of Sam's "Autobiography," *Crashing Thunder* (1926); and, finally, some
autobiographical fragments from Jasper Blowsnake in *The
Road of Life and Death* (1945), an account of the Winnebago Medicine Rite. Radin seems to have collected *all*
the material on which these publications were based in the
years 1908–1913, during which time, as I have noted, he
worked among the Winnebago. Many of Radin's field notes
and transcriptions from this period have been preserved and
are among the papers that were donated by his widow, Doris
Radin, to the American Philosophical Society Library in
1960. These are cataloged in John F. Freeman's *A Guide
to Manuscripts Relating to the American Indian in the Library of the American Philosophical Library* (Philadelphia,
1966). Among these is an item listed as "Sam Blowsnake's
Autobiography" (Freeman, #3897). This consists of three
"American Chief" notebooks (ruled, with yellow covers,
each with a picture of an Indian, bow in hand, and three
tepees in the background!), numbered 30, 31, and 32, and
filled with pencil script in the Winnebago language; each

notebook is dated October 9, 1913, and each is marked, on the cover, "Jasper Blowsnake's Autobiography," with the name Jasper crossed through in pen, and the name Sam written above it. Whose markings are these? Did Radin himself have trouble keeping Sam and Jasper apart in his mind? Unlike many of the other manuscripts in the Radin collection, these notebooks do not have interlinear or facing page translations, and I cannot read Winnebago. Are these notebooks all or part of S. B.'s own manuscript? And, what is actually in them? A transcription and translation of "Sam Blowsnake's Autobiography" is only one of the tasks that remains for the student of *Crashing Thunder* and of Paul Radin's work in Native American autobiography.

A comparison of the autobiographical texts Radin published between 1913 and 1945, together with an examination of his papers in the American Philosophical Library collection, reveal instances of what appear to be the multiple attribution of materials, of overlappings of materials, and— most clearly of all—changes in the published versions of apparently similar materials over the years.

In the 1913 "Personal Reminiscences," Jasper Blowsnake provides no account of his fasting experiences; in *The Winnebago Tribe*, however, there is a monologue called "J. B.'s Fasting Experience." This begins, "I fasted all the time. We moved back to a place where all the leaders used to give their feasts. Near the place where we lived there were three lakes and a black hawk's nest . . ." (*WT*, p. 308). The third chapter of Sam's 1920 "Autobiography" is called "Fasting." Its second paragraph begins, "After a while we got fairly well started on our way back. I fasted all the time. We moved back to a place where all the leaders used to give their feasts. Near the place where we lived there were three lakes and a black hawk's nest . . ." (A, p. 6). This is supposed to be Sam; but his account parallels, detail for detail, and almost word for word, the account ascribed to J. B.; this is carried over into *Crashing Thunder* (*CT*, pp. 17–20) with only a few changes. If this account actually derives from Sam, it is unclear why Radin would have assigned it to Jasper in *The Winnebago Tribe*. That it does indeed come from Sam is suggested by a series of undated manuscript notes Radin made for a commentary on "The Autobiography" (Freeman, #3881) in which he comments on Sam's fasting experience.

In the fifth of these manuscript notes, Radin remarked that:

> Blowsnake's account of his puberty/fasting is not told in a very coherent fashion, and is at times vague and careless. . . . That he should say that he made his appeal to the spirits when the sun rose seems strange to me for that is the moment when one is generally supposed to stop fasting. Blowsnake, I think through an oversight, uses the word for Thunderbirds instead of spirits here.

This is consistent with Radin's footnote in "The Autobiography" that Sam's fasting experience in its "supernatural" details was ". . . peculiar in a number of respects" (A, n. 7). (There is no similar note accompanying the account in *Crashing Thunder*.) Radin's manuscript notes also comment that:

> The fasting experience given here differs considerably from the one told me by Blowsnake's older brother and which was also supervised by his father. This raises the important question of what it is Blowsnake is giving here and whether this is even

approximately what his father had told him. These are difficult questions to answer. My impression is that Blowsnake is probably combining here what his father had told him with the fasting experiences of others, particularly of his brother-in-law [Thunder-Cloud]. It should be remembered that *he himself had not had the experience he here records* and this would permit secondary embellishment to creep in more easily [my emphasis].

We are left, thus, with several questions. Why did Radin assign Sam's fasting experience (as I suspect he did) to J. B. in *The Winnebago Tribe?* If the fasting experience Sam narrated or wrote down was not one he had actually had, but, instead, a composite, replete with "secondary embellishment," why didn't Radin, in the introductory material and notes to "The Autobiography" and *Crashing Thunder,* permit "the important question of what it is Blowsnake is giving here" to surface? Further, if Sam's experience is in some regards "peculiar," how does that observation accord with Radin's purpose, as stated in the introduction to "The Autobiography," of having "some *representative* middle-aged individual . . . describe his life in relation to the social group in which he had grown up" (A, p. 2, my emphasis)? In *Crashing Thunder,* the apparently representative Sam has become a quite extraordinary "rake" (CT, p. x), a most "definite personage" (A, p. 2)—yet still doing duty, it would seem, as just the "real" Indian.

The issue of representativeness and uniqueness, of the conflation of personal-historical experience with collective and conventional experience in a tribal culture is presented as well by Radin's expansion of the "Fasting" chapter of "The Autobiography" for *Crashing Thunder.* In *Crashing Thunder,* Radin added the stories "Crashing Thunder's"

father had told him of his ancestors Weshgishega and Job-
enangiwinxga. But the story of Wecgícega comes from chapter 1 of the "Personal Reminiscences," "How One of My
Ancestors was Blessed by Earth-Maker." There, Jasper's account reads:

> Wecgícega they called him. A Winnebago he was. When he
> was grown up, his father coaxed him to fast; (saying) that when
> Earth-Maker created the various spirits, as many good spirits
> as he made, all of them did he place in control of some-
> thing . . . (PR, p. 294)

In *Crashing Thunder*, not Jasper's but Sam's autobiography,
we have "Fasting: The Story of My Ancestor Weshgishega":

> When Weshgishega was growing up his father coaxed him to
> fast. He told him that Earthmaker had created the various
> spirits, all the good ones he had created, were placed in charge
> of something . . . (CT, p. 20)

Another version of this material appeared in an unidentified
monologue in *The Winnebago Tribe* called "How Wegi'ceka
Tried to See Earthmaker." It begins as follows:

> Once there was a Winnebago whose name was Wegi'ceka. As
> soon as he was grown up his father begged him to fast. The
> old man told his son that Earthmaker, when he created this
> earth, made many good spirits and that he put each one of
> them in control of powers with which they could bless human
> beings. (WT, p. 291)

Radin's note explains that "Some religious experiences" of
the Winnebago "have been cast in a literary form and handed

down from one generation to another. The literary mold in which they have been cast does not in the least interfere with their value as excellent examples of personal experiences . . ." (*WT*, n. 291). This parallels Radin's note in the "Personal Reminiscences," that the Wecgícega story "is really a favorite story among the Winnebago" (*PR*, n. 294), and may or may not actually refer to one of Jasper's historical ancestors. But the interaction of literary convention and individual "personal experience" is a much more complicated matter than Radin allows for. If, as is altogether possible, three different informants (Jasper, Sam, and an unidentified Winnebago) told the same story, in approximately the same words, mingling traditional motifs with their own historical experiences, this would be interesting to know. Yet Radin's tendency to attribute a single narrative to several different narrators may make one wary. I would remark, too, that if Sam Blowsnake has here told the same story as Jasper and another Winnebago, in this instance he appears coherent, precise, and careful in the transmission of traditional material.

Speaking of his brother-in-law, Thunder-Cloud, in the "Personal Reminiscences," Jasper said, "He had lived once long ago, had joined the Medicine Dance and had strictly adhered to all its precepts. A good man he was; no one did he dislike; never did he steal; and never did he fight" (*PR*, p. 303). "Crashing Thunder's" version in 1926 (this did not appear in the 1920 "Autobiography") reads, "Thus my brother-in-law had lived long ago, had joined the Medicine Dance and adhered strictly to its precepts. He was a good man; he disliked no one; he never stole and never did he fight" (*CT*, p. 7). Jasper's conclusion was, "For all these things, I used to love my brother-in-law. Never did I show any disrespect to him . . ." (*PR*, p. 312). "Crashing Thunder's"—Sam's—conclusion reads, "My brother loved Thunder Cloud for these reasons" (*CT*, p. 14). The brothers may well have related the same facts—but, again, did they use exactly the same, or nearly the same, words? In *The Road of Life and Death*, Jasper is presented as saying, "For all these things, I loved my brother-in-law. Never did I show any disrespect toward him" (*RLD*, p. 4). But there Radin drops out a paragraph written by Jasper in which he testifies that "Now that [he is] a Peyote follower," he knows "there was no foundation to what [Thunder-Cloud] said" (*PR*, p. 312). Obviously the dramatic quality of the Medicine Rite would be undercut by an explicit statement of its falsity. "Crashing Thunder's" comments on the falsity of the old ways are also saved for much later in his account. These changes are Radin's.

Thunder-Cloud's own fasting experiences appeared in the middle of chapter 3 of the "Personal Reminiscences": "Then he [Thunder-Cloud] told of his fasting experience" (*PR*, p. 306). There follows some three pages of first-person monologue in quotation marks (i.e., Thunder-Cloud is represented as speaking for himself and in his own words). Thunder-Cloud's narrative is exactly the same as the one that appears in *The Winnebago Tribe* as "Thunder-Cloud's fasting experience" (*WT*, pp. 275–276). [This is also introduced by the unassigned sentence, "Then he (Thunder-cloud) told of his fasting experience."] Radin uses a footnote in the "Personal Reminiscences," to explain that "This is the fasting experience told by all those who have been blessed with shamanistic powers" (*PR*, n. 306). This fasting experience is not given for Thunder-Cloud by Sam in his "Autobiography," although *Crashing Thunder* does contain a portion of the same fasting experience (*CT*, pp. 8–9), this time with changes in the wording that did not appear before. Apparently this is one of the "things" "Crashing Thunder" told Radin "on previous occasions . . . inserted in its proper" place (*CT*, p. xi). Or could it be something told Radin by Thunder-Cloud, or something written by Jasper Blowsnake attributed to Sam?

Radin added to chapter 3, "Fasting," of "The Autobiography" the story of "Crashing Thunder's" brother J.'s blessing. Page 8 of "The Autobiography" reads, "Just then my older brother came home and they objected to his return for he had not been blessed." *Crashing Thunder* repeats this (*CT*, p. 27), but adds, "My brother J., however, obtained a blessing." There follows a third-person, shortened version of the first-person narrative called "Account of J.'s fasting" in *The Winnebago Tribe* (*WT*, pp. 293–295). Who is J.? There were four Blowsnake brothers, and *The Winnebago Tribe* prints narratives both from J. and from J. B. If J. spoke or wrote the account of his fasting given in *The Winnebago Tribe*, was it also repeated verbatim by Sam? It would be interesting to know, for the answer might aid our understanding of the transmission of traditional materials in an oral culture also using written forms.

Similar confusions, overlappings, and multiple attributions occur in Radin's various presentations of the climactic moment in each of the Blowsnake brothers' lives, the moment of their conversion to the Peyote religion. The monologue titled, "J. B.'s Peyote experiences" in *The Winnebago Tribe* (*WT*, pp. 400–412) is almost word for word the same as what appears in chapters 28–34 of Sam's "Autobiography." Peyote conversions by this time had a certain tradition among the Winnebago and individual conversions may have followed a conventionalized pattern. Nonetheless, it seems hard to believe that Jasper and Sam can have had exactly the same experiences (especially, as I note just below, when other, quite nontraditional experiences are assigned to both of them), and have narrated them in exactly the same words. Connected with but not strictly a part of the conversion experience of the Blowsnakes is a murder that both of them are alleged to have committed. In "J. B.'s account of his conversion" in *The Winnebago Tribe* (WT, pp. 412–414), an account which is carried into *The Road of Life and Death* (RLD, pp. 46–49), Jasper—apparently—says, "I was at the old agency. There they were to try me for murder." Sam's arrest and trial for the murder of a Pottawatommie was presented in some detail in "The Autobiography" (A, pp. 41–47) and in *Crashing Thunder* (CT, pp. 148–151, 159–167), and it is referred to by Mountain Wolf Woman, his sister (MWW, pp. 100, 124); but only in this particular monologue is there any indication that Jasper was also in jeopardy for murder. It seems hard not to conclude that this is simply a multiple attribution, the result of carelessness—or some other reason of which I am not aware.

Radin's treatment of Sam's conversion to the peyote religion in "The Autobiography" and in *Crashing Thunder* is also interesting to consider. In "The Effects of the Peyote," chapter 30 of "The Autobiography," Sam writes, "John Rave, the leader, was to conduct the (ceremony)" (A, pp. 55–56). Chapter 31 of *Crashing Thunder* has the same title and repeats the sentence I have just quoted. But whereas "The Autobiography" continues, "I ate five peyote" (A, p. 56), *Crashing Thunder* inserts, "He [John Rave] told of his conversion" (CT, p. 179). There follows a lengthy narrative called "John Rave's Conversion to the Peyote Religion" (CT, pp. 279–285). This is a modified translation of "John Rave's account of the Peyote cult and of his conversion" in *The Winnebago Tribe* (WT, pp. 389–394). (This occurs as "John Rave's peyote experience" in the Radin manuscript collection [Freeman, #3878], with an interlinear translation. Both the versions, in *The Winnebago Tribe* and in *Crashing Thunder,* have claims to accuracy as compared to this rough translation, although they are stylistically different.)

The effect of this insertion into the text of *Crashing Thunder* is to make Sam's account of his conversion much more dramatic than it was in "The Autobiography," for here we are given John Rave not only leading the peyote ceremony but also testifying, at that particular ceremony, to his own conversion. In *Crashing Thunder,* it is only after Rave's narrative that Sam announces, "When John Rave had finished I ate five peyote" (*CT,* p. 186). There is at least the implication that Rave's powerful story may have operated as a cause of S. B.'s own conversion. To the extent that this is so, it is Radin, not Sam Blowsnake, who has produced this effect, for it occurs only in *Crashing Thunder.* This part of *Crashing Thunder,* I would add, appears therefore to be a fiction; John Rave's account is no doubt authentic, and Sam Blowsnake no doubt heard it on one occasion or another. But probably not on this occasion, else its omission from "The Autobiography" is inexplicable.

I save for final—and quite brief—mention the very many small changes Radin made in the titles and arrangements of chapter headings and of the wording as he went from "The Autobiography" to *Crashing Thunder.* There are a good many more than I shall note, but an exhaustive catalog seems to no particular point: whether the various changes are or are not significant must depend upon any given interpreter's aims and outlook. For example, chapter 4 of "The Autobiography" is called "Boyhood Reminiscences"; chapter 4 of *Crashing Thunder* is called "Reminiscences of Childhood." In 1920, chapter 19 is "Continued Dissipation"; this becomes chapter 21 in 1926 and is called "Dissipation." Changes of this nature tell me very little; however, I would remark the fact that chapter 14 in 1920 is called "Brother's Death," whereas the same chapter, now chapter 18 of *Crashing Thunder*, becomes "My Brother Is Murdered," a rather more dramatic title.

I have remarked above Radin's changes in the "Finale" of *Crashing Thunder*, where the sentence in "The Autobiography" that reads "This is the work that was assigned to me" (A, p. 67) became "This is the work predestined for me to do" (*CT*, p. 203). The brief "Finale" has many other changes of this sort. As Nancy Lurie has noted (*MWW*, p. 98), Radin deleted the phrase in "The Autobiography" that read "Then my brother had us do this work . . ." (A, p. 67). Lurie offered no explanation for this deletion; my own conjecture regarding this—Radin's increasing desire to obscure the traces of his participation—has been stated. These and the many other differences between the texts of "The Autobiography" and *Crashing Thunder* mean that it cannot be the case, as Ruth Underhill too readily granted, that "every word of it [*Crashing Thunder*] came out of the Indian's mouth."[22] In any event, whatever words may have come out of "Crashing Thunder's" mouth, those are not the words we readers have. We have no one's spoken words, however much we may be urged to believe that the Indian has been allowed to speak for himself, but only written words, and words in English. Some of these may be J. B.'s, or J.'s words, or Thunder-Cloud's, and most, in some measure, are the interpreter Oliver Lamere's words. But all of these words ultimately are Paul Radin's words. For the final text is his; he is the one who arranged and retranslated, who inserted, deleted, and cued our attention to a range of Western literary models to guide our understanding of these words. This is not to say that Paul Radin made any of it up, but only that, in collaboration with "Crashing Thunder" and a number of other Winnebago, he made it. That "fact" must be dealt with as we proceed to any "interpretation"— a literary or a scientific reading—of the text; to say this, it has been my point throughout, is already to have commenced the interpretive act.

5 /

Yellow Wolf and Black Elk:

History and Transcendence

By the time Paul Radin published *Crashing Thunder*, a considerable change in American thought about the Indian was under way which would achieve legislative expression in the Wheeler-Howard or Indian Reorganization Act (IRA) of 1934. Passed at the urging of FDR's Commissioner of Indian Affairs, John Collier, a social scientist and an admirer of Native American cultures, the IRA sought to legitimate rather than to destroy traditional lifeways. As passed into law and administered under the watchful eye of the Bureau of Indian Affairs, the Act unfortunately tried to secure the Indian determination of Indian affairs through the impo-

Yellow Wolf, October, 1908. Courtesy of the Historical Photographs Collection of Washington State University Libraries, Pullman, Washington.

sition of Western parliamentary forms. This was a bitter paradox at best and, at worst, led to consequences altogether the reverse of Collier's intent. Nonetheless, after Wheeler-Howard, the americanizers' attempt to turn the American Indian into the Indian American no longer had a basis in federal law.

By the 1930s as well, the social sciences in America were firmly entrenched in the university. Sociology and anthropology still tended warily to observe certain territorial distinctions (Durkheim's installation as the Father of Functionalism did not come until somewhat later and was of more interest to British than American anthropologists). Psychology and anthropology were, however, increasingly frequent guests on each other's demesne. Margaret Mead specified 1934, the date of the Hanover interdisciplinary seminar, as the moment of her engagement with psychoanalysis, and seminars under the direction of the neo-Freudian Abram Kardiner in 1936 and 1937 were attended by the anthropologists Edward Sapir, Ruth Benedict, Ruth Bunzel, and Ralph Linton, among others. John Dollard of Yale University, who had been influenced by Karen Horney and Erich Fromm, also worked with Mead; Dollard's influence on social-scientific Indian autobiographies came directly through his book, *Criteria for the Life History*, published in 1935. The conjunction of psychology and anthropology in this later "research investment in culture and personality," as Marvin Harris acutely observes, "exemplifies the attraction of mentalistic and individualistic themes in American social science," and a further turn from history.[1]

Or, to put it another way, we may adduce the conclusion of Claude Lévi-Strauss who in 1943 wrote that "The function of primitive biographies is to provide a *psychological* expression of cultural phenomena."[2] More than forty years have passed since that assessment, but Lévi-Strauss's comment may yet provide the most accurate single characterization of many of the social-scientific Indian autobiographies gathered by professionals in the 1930s and 1940s. Lévi-Strauss's remark came in the course of a brief review of Leo Simmons's *Sun Chief: The Autobiography of a Hopi Indian*, "Published for the Institute of Human Relations" of Yale University, a place where there was a great deal of activity attempting to reconcile psychoanalysis with behavior-and-learning theory. Simmons, working in this self-consciously theoretical context, provided for his book an introduction explaining "The Project and the Procedure," and a set of appendices under the heading, "Concerning the Analysis of Life Histories," in which he elaborated a method called "situational analysis." In regard to this procedural and interpretative apparatus, it was Lévi-Strauss's conclusion that ". . . Simmons' laborious attempt to present a sample of what he expects from the study of life histories does not add very much to the plain, matter-of-fact account of Don's [the Sun Chief's] diary."[3] I believe this to be true. Simmons's apparatus, in some measure like Dollard's "criteria," seems either to elaborate the obvious or to reduce the complexity of the phenomena to the capacities of the theory. Simmons's account of "situational analysis," for example, proceeds to Don Talayesva's life by way of an analogy to "a rat in a grilled cage," and the belief that "Limited situations" could be selected from an individual's life, "expressed in terms of well-defined problems, and interpreted by the aid of sound principles of conditioning."[4] From our present vantage point, it seems hardly necessary to elaborate the difficulties inherent in such formulations.

In any event, whatever researchers in culture and personality may have thought they were doing, they did produce a considerable number of fine autobiographical documents in the thirties and forties—so many, indeed, that Clyde Kluckhohn undertook to study "The Personal Document in Anthropological Science" as part of a larger project of the Social Science Research Council (1945).[5] Shortly before his death, Boas had written that "Autobiographies . . . are of limited value for the particular purpose for which they are being collected," and that "They are valuable rather as useful material for a study of the perversion of truth brought about by the play of memory with the past."[6] Kluckhohn, to the contrary, concluded that there was indeed considerable scientific potential for personal documents. What was important was the clarification and systematization of methods and records, the full enunciation of the procedures employed, and the publication, in whatever form feasible, of notes, transcriptions, and translations.

Whether their interests were primarily cultural or psychological, whether they worked from a highly specific theoretical perspective or from a more generalized curiosity, all the professional anthropologists who took Indian lives in print in this period focused on private individuals. To my knowledge, no one of them sought out any of the world-historical figures—men and women who had participated in or witnessed epochal events—for accounts of their lives. In some measure, the mentalistic and individualistic orientation of American anthropology, its development of culture and personality as an "American version of synchronic

functionalism" (the characterization is Marvin Harris's) ne-
cessitated this choice.[7] And it is obvious that battles and
treaties cannot be the primary focus of the anthropologist.
But surely their context could be; I mean the cultural factors
that had a bearing on when and where and how a battle
was fought, or why some treaties seemed acceptable and
others did not. This might well have been conceived to fall
within the anthropologist's province. Further, who can say
whether the Lakota, Runs-the-Enemy, Red Cloud, and
Dewey Beard—the first two interviewed in 1909, and the
third as late as 1935—tired of telling what they had done
and seen in the Custer Fight, might not have responded to
a request to recall their childhood games and toys, their
visions and powers, their wives and children, and the like?[8]
Surely any one of these men was as representative of the
"real" Sioux as "Crashing Thunder" was of the "real" Winnebago—and with as many problems of transition from the
old life to the new. But the professionals of science did not
work with these people, leaving their stories to be recorded,
to the extent that they were recorded, by amateurs interested
in history.

So far as a generalization may be warranted, it would
appear that the anthropologists tended to structure their
materials according to some variant of either the ironic
pattern I have traced in Barrett's *Geronimo,* or the comic
pattern of Radin's *Crashing Thunder.* This is to affirm what
I have assumed throughout, that the structure of Indian
autobiography is ultimately the responsibility of the Euramerican editor. Certainly it is of considerable interest how
the Native American subject understood and presented his
or her life; but whether we can infer this from the produced

text is very much open to question. After all, we do not have the transcripts of Black Hawk's and Geronimo's original dictation; and the manuscript "Crashing Thunder" composed at Radin's request remains to be retranslated. Further, an adequate terminology for the structures of Native American narratives has yet to be developed. Whereas Western culture structures narrative in the four modes traditionally designated as romance, tragedy, comedy, and irony, these modes are by no means operative in non-Western cultures. Functionally, it would appear, all narrative modes in all cultures show marked similarities, serving to educate and socialize their audiences; structurally, however, there are no such marked similarities.

As David Brumble has recently shown, "Crashing Thunder" himself may have presented his life to Radin as a dramatic confession, for *confessio* as a form had entered Winnebago culture before it was proposed to "Crashing Thunder" or imposed on his text by Paul Radin.[9] Nonetheless, Radin, who clearly felt free to rearrange, retranslate, add and subtract from "Crashing Thunder's" written manuscript, could easily have worked the text in the direction of emphases different from those compatible with the comic mode—had he been so inclined. What we most surely know from Indian autobiography is how the editor understood the Indian's life.

Walter Dyk's *Left-Handed: Son of Old Man Hat*, for example, "unsurpassed" for the "intrinsic quality of the document," in Kluckhohn's judgment,[10] is an instance of scientific discourse in the ironic mode; its subject seems merely to live through one episode of his life after another. To the nonprofessional Western reader, these episodes may appear ordinary and uninteresting or, indeed, extraordinary and quite fascinating (or both). But whatever one's estimate, the events of Left-Handed's life are presented as simply the facts of the case, the things that just happened to happen. This ironic presentation, I believe, helps to explain why it is that the sequel to *Son of Old Man Hat,* published after Dyk's death by his wife, Ruth, seems neither necessary nor anticlimactic. *Left-Handed: A Navajo Autobiography* (1980) contains more than five hundred pages in which only three years of Left-Handed's life in the 1880s are treated. Here, the massiveness of the detail is itself ironic in its effect— but, given the ironic presentation (as I think it) offered by Dyk in the original volume, on what principle could his wife, editing the unused material, select or cut anything? To the extent possible to any text, *Left-Handed* seems to give us everything of its subject's life—with the consequent effect that no one thing seems much more important than any other.

Gilbert Wilson's Hidatsa subject, Edward Goodbird, however, is presented to us as a man who has taken the Christian teachings of the whites as a sure guide to a suc- cessful life in this world. Salvation and the next world, what Goodbird seems to mean by "knowing God," are surely important, but there is a balance between the religious and social dimensions; in a standard, nineteenth-century, Prot- estant way, for Goodbird, prosperity in this world and sal- vation in the next are consistent and not antithetical. The last pages of Goodbird's narrative offer the following observations:

> We Hidatsas know that our Indian ways will soon perish; but we feel no anger. The government has given us a good reser- vation, and we think the new way better for our children. . . .

For myself, my family and I own four thousand acres of land; and we have money coming to us from the government. I own cattle and horses. I can read English, and my children are in school.

I have good friends among the white people, Mr. Hall and others, and best of all, I think each year I know God a little better.

I am not afraid.[11]

For Goodbird, the loss of the old can be accepted without pain or "anger"; his view is optimistic and progressive, a sober but cheerful reconciliation to what the future—on earth, and also, no doubt, in heaven—holds. *Goodbird the Indian,* in some ways like *Crashing Thunder,* works toward the typical conclusions of the comic mode.

A similar comic pattern of integration and reconciliation appears in Leo Simmons's story of Don Talayesva's life, to which I have already referred. Unlike Goodbird, Don draws back from early temptations to christianization and "civilization" in order to reestablish his identity as a Hopi. For Don, the ultimate demonstration of Hopi-ness is to be a father raising his son in proper, traditional fashion. Whatever unconscious anxieties, fears, and longings Don may project onto his adopted son, Norman; whatever the alleged homosexual dynamics of Don's dreams: these must not be divorced from their socio-historical context, from Don's firm insistence on the satisfactions of Hopi identity. Simmons concludes Don's story with a happy dream of prosperity that gives Don "a pleasant future to look forward to."[12] When his life is over, Don hopes "to die in [his] sleep and without any pain. Then . . . to be buried in the Hopi way."[13] Don's return to the old, like "Crashing Thunder's" and Goodbird's turn to the new, is structured in the Western mode of comedy.

For Sam Blowsnake, the Winnebago, Edward Goodbird, the Hidatsa, Don Talayesva, the Hopi, and thousands of other Native Americans, the first third of the twentieth century was an enormously difficult period, one which saw painful strategic splits develop between traditional and progressive factions. To adhere to the old ways, to reject them for new ways, to find some kind of communal and personal reconciliation of the two—or simply to live out one's days: these were the choices. Don Talayesva became a Hopi again; Edward Goodbird became a Christian; Sam Blowsnake joined the peyote church with its admixture of Native and Christian elements: all found they could, in Blowsnake's phrase, "get along nicely." Their stories are comic in structure. Left-Handed (along with many others we have not considered), as we have his story, seems to have lived from day to day, nicely or badly, as it happened: his book is ironic in structure.

But then there are the stories of those Indians who would not enthusiastically embrace the new, yet could not, for all their intense longing, live the old: these potentially tragic narratives do not appear among the texts of the anthropologists.[14] For the tragic form of Indian autobiography we must return to history—as for its romantic form, the mode of worldly transcendence, we must leave both social science and history, rooted as they are in the material world, and turn to a religious poet.

Meeting Black Hawk in 1832, shortly after the Indian Removal Act, J. B. Patterson set to editing the old warrior's autobiography in the interest of historical justice; nonetheless, he largely shared his period's view of the iron "law" of history which posited the progressive triumph of "civilization" over "savagery," and so he structured Black Hawk's decline and fall in the comic mode. S. M. Barrett met Geronimo in 1904 during a time when Indian policy, after the Dawes Act, was committed to americanizing the Indian. Barrett wrote Geronimo's autobiography to complete the historical and scientific/cultural record; interested only in recording the "facts," Barrett structured Geronimo's decline and fall in the ironic mode. Paul Radin, a professional anthropological scientist, met Sam Blowsnake in 1908, still in the Dawes period, and wrote his autobiography as part of the overall effort of anthropological salvage. Neither a "civilized" Indian nor the "romantic" Indian of the James Fenimore Cooper type, Blowsnake seemed a successful reconciliation of the old and the new; thus his story is also structured as comedy. Lucullus Virgil McWhorter met the Nez Perce warrior Yellow Wolf in 1907. But McWhorter did not publish Yellow Wolf's story until 1940, in the period when government policy recognized the dignity and worth of Native cultures. It was possible, then, to speak seriously, as John Collier and others did, of how much "civilization" had to learn from the Indian—or at least it was possible to speak that way in Washington, D.C., in New York, or in New Haven. But McWhorter, a free lance unattached to any government agency or university, was a westerner. And, where he came from, his neighbors, pioneers and sons of pioneers, did not share eastern enthusiasm for the Indian and his ways.

In 1877, the Nez Perce had been ordered to exchange the million or so acres they held in the Wallowa country of what is now eastern Oregon for some twelve hundred acres on the Lapwai reservation in present-day Idaho. Although Young Joseph, their principal peace chief, sought to comply, a series of events caused him, along with Looking Glass and other traditional Nez Perce leaders, to resolve on an escape to Canada, where they hoped to join Sitting Bull and his Sioux. The flight of the Nez Perce took four months and covered thirteen hundred miles, only to end a mere thirty miles short of the Canadian border. In October of 1877, Joseph surrendered to Colonel Nelson Miles who had been dispatched to the aid of General O. O. Howard, Joseph's foremost pursuer. A warrior known for his skill at horsebreaking, Yellow Wolf, twenty-one years old in 1877, was an active participant in the entire campaign. He did not surrender with Joseph but slipped off to Canada with Chief White Bird.

In relation to this episode in history, McWhorter's sympathies lie entirely with the Nez Perce traditionalists. Unlike J. B. Patterson who disclaimed responsibility for the viewpoints expressed in Black Hawk's autobiography, unlike S. M. Barrett who claimed to let the reader draw his own conclusions, McWhorter makes his position militantly clear from the very start. The dedication to his book reads:

> To the shades of patriotic warriors, heroic women, feeble age, and helpless infancy—sacrificed on the gold-weighted altars of Mammon and political chicanery, 1863–77, are these pages most fervently inscribed.[15]

For all of McWhorter's explicit partisanship, however, he is by no means indifferent to objective truth. To this end, he will document the opinions of others beside Yellow Wolf and the Nez Perce regarding the events of 1877, and document as well his own participation in the making of Yellow Wolf's story.

Thus each chapter of McWhorter's book begins with a headnote indicating the circumstances of the narration to follow, dating and placing the story of the story. There are also internal breaks in the chapters in which McWhorter describes such things as pauses of noteworthy length, hesitations, tones of voice, gestures, or "style" (as when McWhorter comments that Yellow Wolf's narration of the Nez Perces' final battle was delivered "with an unusual degree of rhetoric" [p. 212]). McWhorter's headnote to chapter 3, "The Battle of White Bird Canyon," for example, concludes:

> We walked to the more southern of the two Cemetery Buttes, where, in the preceding chapter, we saw the Indians gathered. The climb to its summit so taxed the old warrior's strength that he was compelled to take a short rest. Then for several minutes he stood silently gazing over the broken country to the west. Pointing across to the southern base of the highest ridge-like butte, he took up the trend of his narrative as follows: . . . (p. 54)

Or, early in chapter 5, "The Fight with Captain Randall's Volunteers," we have McWhorter speaking in his own voice:

> Wanting to obtain the Nez Perce version of the status of Chief Looking Glass at the outbreak of hostilities, I interposed, "General Howard states that some of Looking Glass's men had joined Chief Joseph's band before this time, either before you crossed the Salmon or while you were south of that river." To this came the quick response: . . . (p. 78)

In chapter 2, it turns out to be a handclasp between McWhorter and Yellow Wolf (p. 47) at a particularly anxious juncture of the narrative that permits it to continue. This procedure is followed throughout.

McWhorter's technique constitutes what the Russian Formalists, his contemporaries, referred to as a "baring of the device," a refusal to naturalize what is, after all, art(ful); or, in the terminology I have earlier employed, a discovery rather than a concealment of the traces of production of the text. Yellow Wolf's "own story" could not only be his *own* story, and McWhorter refuses to create the illusion that it could be, that it is. Not a discourse of *assujettissement*, of subjugation, this is, as we shall see further, a discourse of equalization. (We might note also that McWhorter's openness in this regard begins to meet one of Clyde Kluckhohn's criteria for scienticity.)[16]

What is especially important to remark is that McWhorter's procedure insists upon the performed quality of Yellow Wolf's story.[17] Unlike those editors of Indian autobiography who strove to produce a *text* that would *read* as a smooth and seamless verbal object, McWhorter does not let us forget that this text is a recitation, with all the gaps and fissures of what we have come to call everyday discourse. McWhorter's concern for what he heard, for the dramatic, oral, and immediate quality of Yellow Wolf's narrative—with, as I have said, its pauses, changes of tone and volume, and the like—looks forward to the efforts of Dennis Tedlock and Jerome Rothenberg rather than back to those of the older historians and anthropologists.

McWhorter, of course, is not only—not even primarily—interested in the rhetorical, affective power of Yellow Wolf's narration but in its truth. Thus, as already noted, he must permit others besides Yellow Wolf and himself to speak, giving them the opportunity to confirm or contest the Nez Perce perspective. This broadens the definition of authorship with which McWhorter works to include a wide range of relevant others both from his own tribe and from Yellow Wolf's. The book includes notes and appendices (to individual chapters as well as to the text in its entirety) which quote widely and at length from the published and unpublished testimony of participants in and eyewitnesses to the events in question. Perhaps the majority of these quotations come from General Howard and Colonel Miles, adversaries and conquerors of the Nez Perce. McWhorter also quotes from official government reports, from the published and unpublished letters and documents of army officers, and from responses to his own specific queries. Not all of these, by any means, are sympathetic to the Nez Perce. McWhorter's movement, then, is away from monologic presentation and univocal authority in the direction of—in the sense of Bakhtin, another Russian contemporary—the dialogic. Even autobiography, it may here be seen, is socially constituted, the "I" who speaks a collective construct. To be sure, McWhorter did not learn this from the Russians; rather, he discovered it on the occasion of his first interviews with Yellow Wolf. In his headnote to the second chapter, McWhorter recalls how he was

. . . surprised to see Yellow Wolf and interpreter Hart walking up from the river, accompanied by Two Moons, Roaring Eagle, and Chief David Williams, all of the Joseph band. These men came and sat through each day's session, mostly in silence, but there was an occasional short conference held in their own language. It was not until afterwards that I learned it was customary to have witnesses to what was said. The listeners, should

they detect error, intentional or otherwise, in statements, were
privileged to make corrections. (p. 34)

This was the custom, not, to be sure, for autobiography as
such, which did not exist among the Indians, but for the
telling of coup stories, which were always at one and the
same time individual and collective, original and augmen-
tative in both content and form.

McWhorter's particular collectivization of autobiography
is, then, an adaptation of an indigenous American—a Native American—practice. In *Yellow Wolf*, we find the abandonment of the search for a European model for the
autobiographies of the unlettered begun more than a century
and a half earlier by John Filson. By the time McWhorter
produced his book of Yellow Wolf's life, it had once more
become possible to look to the Indian for a model of the
American self—a self, on this occasion, less dedicated to
"Mammon and political chicanery" than Americans had so
far evolved—and, for the first time, it had become possible
to look to the Indian for a model of the American book as
well. In *Yellow Wolf*, the ideal self implied is one radically
opposed to atomistic individualism, to the privatization of
property and discourse. McWhorter's procedure may thus
be considered in the context of that "revulsion from Americanism" of the twenties and thirties traced by
F. H. Matthews, a context in which there may be found
such diverse and opposed figures as Mary Austin and the
William Carlos Williams of *In the American Grain*, and
the expatriates Ezra Pound and T. S. Eliot as well.[18]

McWhorter's authorial stance and its consequent requirements—headnotes and footnotes, interruptions of the text,

appendices—make for a book in flagrant violation of the statutes of Western esthetics. McWhorter's adoption of something like the Native American mode of collective production, his refusal to produce a seamless narrative, univocal in its authority, have disqualified *Yellow Wolf* from the high opinion of critics whose evaluative standards derive from the modernist and New-Critical traditions. (The same low valuation, of course, is accorded traditional Native American narratives which seem insufficiently unified or cohesive, repetitious or rambling, and so on.)

Moving from S. B.'s 1920 "Autobiography" to the 1926 *Crashing Thunder,* Paul Radin reduced the number of his footnotes, rearranged the materials, and composed an introduction which sought to place *Crashing Thunder* in the company of texts by Cellini, Voltaire, and Balzac. Asserting the epistemological primacy of science, Radin nonetheless claimed to appropriate the power and status of art for his book. One measure of his success is that *Crashing Thunder*—and with good reason—continues, at least to some extent, to be taught as Native American literature, and also as American social science. *Yellow Wolf,* however, so far as I can judge, is simply not taught at all; occasionally referred to by historians, and—less often—by anthropologists, it is entirely neglected as a type of American literature.[19] Having rejected the conception of the author as a God in his Heaven, exclusively empowered to create, and the conception of the text as handed down from on high, McWhorter has paid a price.

Yet his book has specific and abundant interest as literature and deserves consideration among the texts that define American literature. For, although the form of *Yellow Wolf* (in the sense of the mode of production of the text) and its content (Yellow Wolf's own story as inevitably intertwined with the history of his people) derive, as I have argued, from Native American culture and experience, the structure of the book—what is omitted or included—and its particular emplotment—the arrangement and emphases given the materials—derive from Western culture and are the responsibility of the non-Indian editor. It was McWhorter, after all, who determined to patch together an account of Yellow Wolf's early life, despite his reluctance to speak of it; and he also overcame Yellow Wolf's "reluctance to speak of the aftermath of the war" (p. 229). Yellow Wolf attempted to adhere to the Plains sense of the *coup* story, the story of actions performed in war, as the central meaning of the request to "tell his story." But McWhorter is true to the Western conception of autobiography as the story of a whole life, and it is that conception that prevails. How to structure that life coherently and meaningfully—indeed, what meaning to give it by a particular structural deployment—this central problem of narrative is McWhorter's to solve. Having commenced a *literary* reading of *Yellow Wolf* with a cognitively responsible decision to foreground the mode of production of the signifier, we now pursue that reading by an analysis of the order of the signifier.

McWhorter saw the Nez Perce, as he wrote elsewhere, as "the wilderness gentry of the Pacific Northwest."[20] Seen thus as Nature's noblemen, the Nez Perce, when it came their turn to stand in the way of American expansion and then to be defeated, could readily enough be seen as tragic figures. Indeed, in his introduction to the book, Mc-Whorter, describing Yellow Wolf, writes that "Tragedy was written in every lineament of his face . . ." (p. 14). As McWhorter handles it, the decline and fall of Yellow Wolf and his people eventuates in the same "epiphany of law, of that which is and must be," experienced by Black Hawk and his people, and Geronimo and his.[21] Patterson structured this as the sad comedy of progress in which the red man's decline was but the misfortunate corollary of the white man's—of "civilization's"—ascent. Barrett understood Apache defeat ironically, as merely something that happened many years ago; as America's westward expansion by the turn of the twentieth century had come to include "openings" even into China and Japan, what could be more obvious than the power of civilization? There is no cause for tears, nor either for joy, in Geronimo's story, which is presented strictly for the record.

But McWhorter understands the defeat of the Nez Perce tragically. Yellow Wolf's people, after all, were "sacrificed on the gold-weighted altars of Mammon and political chicanery"; they are the *pharmakoi*, or scapegoats, of "civilization," more sinned against than sinning. Inasmuch as "Mammon" and "political chicanery" define what must be, McWhorter's tragic vision approaches near to that irony which finds the world a place of corruption and absurdity.

McWhorter's tragic structure even contains a well-marked moment of climax, which occurs in chapter 23, "A Voluntary Surrender." Here, Yellow Wolf, after spending time among Sitting Bull's Sioux in Canada, returns to the United States and turns himself in at the Lapwai agency. This "surrender" requires him to face the Nez Perce Indian Agent, John B. Monteith, a man he had come to hate deeply and to blame substantially for the Nez Perce troubles. In a dramatically presented scene, Monteith enters, and, speaking through an interpreter, orders Yellow Wolf, "Look at me!" Yellow Wolf will not (p. 281). The Agent calls Yellow Wolf, aged twenty-one, "a very good boy," and then, as Yellow Wolf tells it, "He walked up to me and shook hands with me. I thought not to touch his hand, but I did" (p. 282). Immediately after, Yellow Wolf is placed in the guard house, soon to be sent off to Indian Territory. It is the physical contact with Monteith, I would suggest, that most powerfully dramatizes Yellow Wolf's submission and recognition of what must be.

This particular emplotment is not given by, or somehow inherent in, the material; rather, it is a function of McWhorter's apprehension of the material. Cyrus Townsend Brady, for example, in a book published originally in 1907, treats the flight of Joseph and his people as "The Epic of the Nez Perces," celebrating the courage and valor of the fighting man, Indian and white, as against the torpor and pusillanimity of the bureaucrat and the civilian.[22] Brady's "Epic" approximates ironic satire. General Howard and Colonel Miles, it might be said, in their various publications dealing with the Nez Perce campaign, tend to mixed forms of comedy and satire, celebrating the triumph of civilization but wary of entrusting its future to civilians.[23] These writers approve the defeat of "savagery" while praising Nez Perce generalship and soldierliness; there is no tragedy to be discerned in their accounts.

McWhorter's tragic presentation of Yellow Wolf's life functions in consonance with federal Indian policy—its intentions, at least—and, generally speaking, the aims of salvage anthropology both of which were anathema to the americanizers and christianizers convinced that Indian "savagery" must fade into the past. McWhorter's book is also an overt challenge to his region's perspective on white-Indian history. For McWhorter researched, wrote, and published in the west where, as late as 1956, there could be objection to honoring Chief Joseph even by naming a dam after him. His viewpoint on the events of 1877 is not that of a substantial number of his contemporaries resident in Idaho and Oregon. And, too, as I have said, *Yellow Wolf* also flies in the face of modernist and New-Critical standards of writing—these deriving considerably from Europe and the American east—which valorize the text as object not performance, removing it from history, and celebrating foremost those individual talents whose original works relate to no history but literary history, or tradition. McWhorter's book is otherwise, tending in this regard not eastward but westward. *Yellow Wolf* is far better appreciated if it is not thought of, in Mary Austin's phrase, as strictly "a thing of type and paper."[24] Out of print for almost half a century, *Yellow Wolf: His Own Story* deserves our continued attention.

Perhaps the single best-known Indian autobiography of all comes neither from the discourse of history nor from that of science. The product of a close association between a Native American visionary and a Euramerican mystic poet, it is *Black Elk Speaks* (1932) which most nearly approximates the religious drama Ruth Underhill took *Crashing Thunder* to be.

It was apparently by accident that John G. Neihardt came to record Black Elk's great vision. By accident—or, as Neihardt believed, by some sort of supernatural direction. In 1930, Neihardt, author of four parts of a projected five-part epic, *The Cycle of the West*, traveled to the Pine Ridge reservation in South Dakota as part of his research for his epic's fifth and final part, *The Song of the Messiah*, which was to deal with the Ghost Dance and Wounded Knee. As Neihardt tells the story, he was greeted by Black Elk as the one who had been sent to preserve and transmit Black Elk's vision and knowledge.

After a time of ritual preparation, Black Elk narrated his story to Neihardt from May 10 to May 28, 1931. Present to participate in the telling in traditional Plains fashion were Fire Thunder, Standing Bear, and Iron Hawk. Black Elk's son Ben, who had studied at the Carlisle Indian School, served as translator; Neihardt's daughter Enid served as stenographer. Her notes and transcripts of the interviews are among Neihardt's papers in the Western Historical Manuscripts Collections of the University of Missouri. They have been examined by Robert Sayre, Sally McCluskey, Michael Castro and, most recently and most perceptively, by Clyde Holler.[25] My own brief discussion is particularly indebted to Holler's work.

Central to Black Elk's life is his extraordinarily vivid and elaborate vision, part of which came to him when he was only five years old, and the greater part when he was nine. After some years of reticence, Black Elk spoke of his vision, which was then performed by his people. The vision was granted to him, Black Elk repeatedly asserts, so that he might keep the sacred hoop of his people unbroken and make the tree flower once more, preserving the traditional culture of the Sioux in the face of the whites' massive assault upon it.

This, Black Elk admits sadly, proved to be impossible. Neihardt has Black Elk conclude his story as follows:

> And I, to whom so great a vision was given in my youth,—
> you see me now a pitiful old man who has done nothing, for
> the nation's hoop is broken and scattered. There is no center
> any longer, and the sacred tree is dead.[26]

Yet, as we now know, this ending as well as the book's lovely beginning were not Black Elk's but John Neihardt's. "The beginning and the ending are mine," Neihardt has written, "they are what [Black Elk] would have said if he had been able. . . . And the translation—or rather the *transformation*—of what was given me was expressed so that it could be understood by the white world."[27] Neihardt has no qualms whatever about speaking for another; but it is very much open to question whether this is indeed what Black Elk "would have said" or, for that matter, whether it is the way he would have chosen to end his story.

In the case of *Black Elk Speaks*, the existence of a rather full record of the Black Elk/Neihardt collaboration makes it possible not only logically to infer Black Elk's own view of his story but empirically to demonstrate it. As Holler has convincingly shown, Black Elk did not at all consider his mission to revive and sustain Lakota culture as over and "dead" at Wounded Knee in 1890; rather, he teaches Neihardt, and prays to the Great Spirit with an unbroken and ongoing concern to make the tree flower once more. "From Black Elk's side," Clyde Holler writes, "the book is a creative response by an eminent Lakota *wicasa wakan* [man of power, wise man] to the religious crisis of his times."[28] Whatever may have died at Wounded Knee, Black Elk and his hopes for his people did not; even in 1931, Black Elk was engaged in traditional ritual means to influence the fate of the Lakota.

This is not at all how Neihardt presented the matter; indeed, he edited and deleted those portions of Black Elk's narration that would emphasize his persisting desire for a return to the old ways. There seem, broadly, two reasons for this. First, Black Elk's view of his life and the life of his people continues to uphold the dream of the Ghost Dancers for a return to a traditional way of life (Holler, pp. 41ff). But Neihardt, for all the mystical overlay, was essentially a christianizer and civilizer of the Dawes–Friends of the Indian type. Much as he deeply responded to aspects of the old Plains religion, Neihardt was no cultural relativist, and he saw the Ghost Dancers' faith in an Indian Messiah as an unmitigated, retrograde error. The Native American future Neihardt envisaged was one of "civilization" and, most particularly, christianization—and Neihardt was determined to appropriate Black Elk's authority for such a view. I can do no better than refer the reader to Clyde Holler's study for a sustained and detailed demonstration of this point. Second, even had Neihardt somehow been willing and able to grasp and to credit the continuous nature of Black Elk's revivalistic efforts, he could not have structurally represented them in narrative.

For just as Neihardt's thought about Indians derives far more from the 1890s than it does from his own period, so, too, does his thought about art. As a poet committed to European forms in a militantly anachronistic fashion—he would be the Virgil or the Milton of the Plains—Neihardt seems to have had no interest whatever in formal experimentation.[29] But that is exactly what was required—what would have been required—for him to tell the story of something *un-ended*. I am saying that Black Elk presented his life to Neihardt not as having achieved full significance in some past event but as currently and actively seeking significance. Indeed, Black Elk's efforts revive hopefully precisely because of Neihardt's intention to tell his story and publish it to the world—gestures Black Elk understood ritualistically and in terms of their potential efficacy. In 1931 Black Elk spoke to Neihardt as an action consistent with past actions, and an attempt yet again to make history.

But Western narrative has no convention for the representation of the ongoing and un-ended; traditionally, Western authors have always sought to provide at least the "sense of an ending," in Frank Kermode's phrase. Such a sense, indeed, acted precisely as a marker differentiating the artistic or fictional text from the texts of "life" or history which do not quite end.[30] In the 1890s and, acutely, after the First World War, the problem of narrative closure presented itself as a major esthetic concern (one, to be sure, that has not gone away)—as the careers of Neihardt's contemporaries Conrad, Pound, Eliot and, most particularly, Franz Kafka illustrate. But Neihardt, determined to write epic, is thoroughly uninterested in this problem. Inasmuch as his conscious convictions required him to assert the death of traditional Lakota lifeways, and inasmuch as he had no interest whatever in experimenting with poetic and narrative forms, he confronts the writing of Black Elk's story as if his only concern were the choice of a particular emplotment.

It is obvious that Black Elk's story could not be structured ironically for it is not, as Neihardt apprehends it, incidental or accidental. Rather, it is intensely significant. What, then, does it signify? The significance cannot be comic because

Black Elk is too clearly short of integration into Christian society; he has not either, of course, managed to feel himself satisfactorily integrated—re-integrated—into the traditional Lakota culture, another comic possibility (but in theory only, so repugnant in practice was this to Neihardt). It is the tragic mode that all the commentators agree has provided structure and significance for *Black Elk Speaks*. But this assessment can stand some further scrutiny.

We may consider the commentary of Michael Castro, a recent student of *Black Elk Speaks*, as exemplary. Castro writes:

> As literature [*Black Elk Speaks*] is tragedy in the greatest sense—a moving human story of declining fortune and ultimate fall from power, *but one with a transcendent vision* which inspires and uplifts all those who read it with understanding.[31]

Unfortunately, the last words of this are something of an empty piety, asserting as they do that the touchstone for "understanding" must be a personal sense of inspiration and uplift, an arbitrary and wholly subjective standard to raise. But the rest is well worth considering. *Black Elk Speaks*, that is, is assuredly a story of decline and fall. But it does not emphasize the "epiphany of law" nor does it urge resignation to "that which is and must be"; instead—Castro is quite correct—it celebrates the transcendence of what is and must be. The mode of transcendence, however, is not tragedy but romance.

Indeed, it is not hard at all to understand Neihardt's need for romantic transcendence. In typical Western fashion, Neihardt's bent is to separate the natural and the supernatural, the social and the religious (a separation that Native American thought does not make). Neihardt, we understand, would very much like to see American society organized so as to reflect the religious values he approves—but he knows perfectly well that it is not, in actuality, so organized. If Neihardt were indeed writing tragedy, he would have had to make Black Elk resign himself to American society as it actually was—as it revealed itself to be at Wounded Knee. But what was revealed at Wounded Knee was the superiority of American power and might; Wounded Knee was a triumph of technology not of value. Neihardt's mystic, Christian desire for, as he put it, "the brotherhood of man and the unity and holiness of all life," his sense of "religious obligation" would not permit him to present *that* superiority as the "law" revealed in *Black Elk Speaks.*[32] It is the vision of American society as it is, the world of material power but spiritual poverty, that Neihardt seeks to transcend.

Thus *Black Elk Speaks* centers on Black Elk's great vision and concludes not with the last word attributed to Black Elk (that word is "dead"), nor with the resignation Neihardt himself has insisted on but, rather, with Neihardt's own last words and a scene of supernatural power. The last chapter of the narration proper in Neihardt's book is followed by an "Author's Postscript." Reassuming the mantle of univocal authorship put off by J. B. Patterson just a hundred years earlier (and being refused at that very moment by L. V. McWhorter), Neihardt presents the drama of Black Elk's return to Harney Peak, "the center of the world," where he had first received his great vision. There, on a clear day, in the midst of a drought, Black Elk asks his power for a bit of rain as a sign of its continued presence, and the power does not fail. This, for Neihardt, is the appropriate conclusion to the story. Black Elk prays:

> . . . "In sorrow I am sending a feeble voice, O Six Powers of
> the World. Hear me in my sorrow, for I may never call again.
> O make my people live!"
>   For some minutes the old man stood silent, with face uplifted,
> weeping in the drizzling rain.
>   In a little while, the sky was clear again. (p. 274)

Is the dream "ended," "dead?" Will the Sioux abandon the "blindness of the old savage religion" (Holler, p. 29), rejecting the Ghost Dance Messiah and accepting the Christ? Whatever the answer, there remains for Neihardt the transcendent power of the "supernormal," before which we must awe-fully pause—no matter what the material efficacy or inefficacy of that power in the material world. It is here that Neihardt places the ultimate emphasis, going beyond material tragedy to the triumphant idealism of romance. It is Black Elk's ongoing capacity to perform miracles, his power, that Neihardt wants to "be understood by the white world" (p. 6).

Like Joyce's Stephen Dedalus, Neihardt perceives "history" as a "nightmare from which [he] is trying to awaken." Neihardt's strategy to escape the bad dream involves not the presumptive objectivity and neutrality of science but the presumptive transcendental capacity of religious romance. Black Elk's book, his story told "through" Neihardt, is not finally tragic—nor is it comic or ironic either; rather, in its valorization of the "supernormal" it is romantic in its emplotment. Neihardt's "Postscript" is the formal equivalent of what Frye describes as the third—and most character-istic—stage of romance, the *anagnorisis*, or "exaltation of the hero."[33] The three stages of romance Frye calls "the *agon* or conflict, the *pathos* or death-struggle, and the *anagnorisis* or discovery, the recognition of the hero, who has clearly proved himself to be a hero even if he does not survive the conflict."[34] Neihardt's "Postscript" confirms Black Elk as "the typical hero of romance," one who is "superior in degree to other men," and, most particularly, "to his environment."[35]

Neihardt's work on Black Elk's story was a labor of America's Great Depression period; the most recent introduction to a new edition of that story by Vine Deloria dates from the late 1970s, the end of a period of social hopefulness.[36] Deloria's voice is also raised in the interest of transcending the social and historical world. He is not in the least interested—"Can it matter?"—in how much of the book comes from Black Elk and how much from John Neihardt (p. xiv). "It is good, . . ." concludes Deloria, "It is enough" (p. xiv). In opting for ignorance, Deloria, like all those who would prefer not to inquire, chooses the status quo: accepting *Black Elk Speaks* with no questions asked, Deloria accepts John Neihardt's version of and prescription for the Native American future. In doing so, he precisely rejects Black Elk's own view of the matter, one that is consistent, as Clyde Holler has effectively shown, with the views of other Lakota traditionalists like Frank Fools Crow, Plenty Wolf, and Lame Deer. It would be a cruel irony indeed if Neihardt's *Black Elk Speaks* became, as Deloria asserts it has, "a North American bible of all tribes" (p. xiii), for if one did actually wish, in Deloria's phrase, to "clarify those beliefs that are 'truly Indian,'" one would need to know rather precisely just what it was that Black Elk himself said.

What Deloria wishes to transcend are "electronic media," and the "machines of a scientific era" (p. xiii) which, he claims, are eroding Indian communities along with "other American communities." This may well be true; but technological developments are not inherently alienating in themselves nor, in any case, does it make sense to fulminate against them once they have made their appearance. To wish to ignore, by somehow rising above, advanced technology is merely to allow its real and human disposition to reside with the powers that be—however destructive they may be.

This is not to disparage the romantic longing for transcendence as such; for the desire of romantic thought to redeem this present world of injustice and pain is shared by materialist and idealist alike. Yet even Northrop Frye acknowledges that "The romance is nearest of all literary forms to the wish-fulfilment dream."[37] And my comments mean only to urge that we historicize romantic desire as a form of utopian thought whose concern is to transcend the world *as presently constituted.* For to desire to transcend all social forms whatever is most assuredly nothing more than a wishful dream, a regressive fantasy.

Indian autobiographies continued to be produced through the 1940s and into our own time; and no doubt there will remain occasions for their production in the future. Nonetheless, to an increasing degree Native Americans for some time already have shown the capacity and will to represent their own lives without the intermediation of the Eur-american—historian, scientist, or poet. And Euramericans concerned with the representation of Indian lives have themselves become more sophisticated and more modest. To the extent that Native Americans retain traditional life-ways and thus retain their distance from Euramerican art forms, we may well see further examples of original bicul-tural composite composition. The fine books of Fools Crow's life, of Lame Deer's, and of Frank Mitchell's, all published in the 1970s, attest to the potential vitality of the genre of Indian autobiography.[38] Nonetheless, any future examples of the genre will appear in a context increasingly domi-nated—at least so far as the white world's awareness is con-cerned—by autobiographies by Indians who, while deeply interested in the old ways, have become extremely sophis-ticated in their manipulation of new—Euramerican, writ-ten—ways. In their different fashions all of these life histories, and those of their predecessors, deserve study and inclusion in the canon of American literature.

Notes

1 / An Approach to Native American Texts

1. Dell Hymes, "Reading Clackamas Texts," in *Traditional American Indian Literatures: Texts and Interpretations*, ed. Karl Kroeber (Lincoln, Nebr., 1981), p. 117.

2. See Dennis Tedlock, ed. and trans., *Finding the Center: Narrative Poetry of the Zuni Indians* (New York, 1972; rpt. Lincoln, Nebr., 1978); and Tedlock, "Toward an Oral Poetics," *New Literary History* 8 (Spring 1977):507–519.

3. Walter J. Ong, S.J., *Interfaces of the Word* (Ithaca, N.Y., 1977), p. 9.

4. Gayatri Chakravorti Spivak, "Revolutions That As Yet Have No Model: Derrida's *Limited Inc*," *Diacritics* 10 (Winter 1980):36.

5. Dennis Tedlock, "On the Translation of Style in Oral Narrative," *Journal of American Folklore* 84 (Jan.-Mar. 1971):118.

6. Ibid., p. 114.

7. Mary Austin, *The American Rhythm: Studies and Reëxpressions of Amerindian Songs* (Boston, 1923; rpt. New York, 1980).

8. See William Brandon, ed., *The Magic World: American Indian Songs and Poems* (New York, 1971); Jerome Rothenberg, ed., *Technicians of the Sacred: A Range of Poetries from Africa, America, Asia & Oceania* (Garden City, N.Y., 1968); and Rothenberg, ed., *Shaking the Pumpkin: Traditional Poetry of the Indian North Americas* (Garden City, N.Y., 1972). Rothenberg and Tedlock edit *Alcheringa*, a journal of ethnopoetics. Although received favorably at first, Rothenberg's practice has increasingly been criticized, most tellingly by William Bevis ("American Indian Verse Translations," *College English* 35 [Mar. 1974]:693–703), and most recently by William M. Clements ("Faking the Pumpkin: On

Jerome Rothenberg's Literary Offenses," *Western American Literature* 16 [Nov. 1981]:193–204).

9. Richard Ohmann, "The Shaping of a Canon: U.S. Fiction, 1960–1975," *Critical Inquiry* 10 (September, 1983):199–223, quotation from p. 204.

10. Jack Goody, *The Domestication of the Savage Mind* (Cambridge, 1977), p. 158.

11. Fredric Jameson, "Marxism and Historicism," *New Literary History* 11 (Autumn 1979):70.

12. Michel Foucault, "What Is an Author?" *Language, Counter-Memory, Practice: Selected Essays and Interviews*, ed. Donald F. Bouchard (Ithaca, N.Y., 1977), p. 124.

13. Ibid., p. 123.

14. John Bierhorst, introduction to *In the Trail of the Wind: American Indian Poems and Ritual Orations*, ed. Bierhorst (New York, 1971), pp. 4–5.

15. Dennis Tedlock, "The Spoken Word and the Work of Interpretation in American Indian Religion," in *Traditional American Indian Literatures*, ed. Karl Kroeber, pp. 47–48.

16. One reason why Indian oratory was initially easier for Euramericans to preserve was that the particular speech seemed to be the discourse of a single prominent individual. Meanwhile, the notion of the great power of the individual Indian orator coexisted all through the nineteenth century with the exasperated recognition of the traditional and formulaic nature, the inevitably social and conventional nature, of any rhetorical act. Thus many of the old Indian fighters recorded their exasperation that one or another "chief" could not come to what they felt was the point without recapitulating the history of his people or invoking the earth as our common mother.

17. Dell Hymes, "Some North Pacific Coast Poems: A Problem in Anthropological Philology," *American Anthropologist* 67 (1965):336. This essay is reprinted with some changes and additions in Hymes's *In Vain I Tried to Tell You: Essays in Native American Ethnopoetics* (Philadelphia, 1981).

18. Frank Kermode, *The Genesis of Secrecy: On the Interpretation of Narrative* (Cambridge, Mass., 1979), p. 99; see also pp. 125–126.

Notes

19. Dell Hymes, "Discovering Oral Performance and Measured Verse in American Indian Narrative," *New Literary History* 8 (Spring 1977):443. See also Hymes's comments on the Indian "author" in his "Breakthrough into Performance," in *Folklore: Performance and Communication*, eds. Dan Ben-Amos and Kenneth S. Goldstein (The Hague, 1975), pp. 11–74.

20. Edward Said, "Reflections on Recent American 'Left' Literary Criticism," *Boundary* 2 8 (Fall 1979):26.

21. Raymond Williams, "Base and Superstructure in Marxist Cultural Theory," in *Problems in Materialism and Culture* (London, 1980), p. 48; all further references to this work will be included in the text.

22. On this, see Tedlock's comments in his introduction to *Finding the Center*, pp. xxv–xxvi, as well as in his "The Spoken Word and the Work of Interpretation," in *Traditional American Indian Literatures*, ed. Karl Kroeber, pp. 48–57.

23. Paul de Man, "The Epistemology of Metaphor," *Critical Inquiry* 5 (Autumn 1978):30.

24. See Lewis Henry Morgan, *Ancient Society; or, Researches in the Lines of Human Progress from Savagery, through Barbarism to Civilization* (1877; New York, 1963).

25. Margot Liberty, "Francis La Flesche: The Osage Odyssey," in *American Indian Intellectuals*, ed. Liberty, Proceedings of the American Ethnological Society, 1976 (Saint Paul, Minn., 1978), p. 52.

26. Raymond Williams, *Marxism and Literature* (London, 1977), p. 46.

27. This account is indebted to Marvin Harris's development of "cultural materialism" in *The Rise of Anthropological Theory* (New York, 1979), and in *Cultural Materialism: The Struggle for a Science of Culture* (New York, 1979) which, with Raymond Williams's "cultural materialism" (as developed particularly in *Marxism and Literature*), has been of great use to me. Neither Harris nor Williams has anything to say about Native American literature nor, to my knowledge, has either commented in print on the other's use of the term "cultural materialism." Addendum: Since the above was written, I have read Terry Eagleton's *Literary Theory: An Introduction* (Minneapolis, 1983), and it occurs to me, as a result, that my call for "science" and "law" may sound either

naive or bloodless or both, leaving only implicit, as it does, what should not only have been explicit but forceful: it is not the theory or law as an end in itself that interests me but its "nontrivial effectivity"—the determination of which involves questions of morality, ideology or, in Eagleton's broad and accurate use of the term, politics. Although I retain the conventional construction, "literary criticism," what I mean by it, as the specific analyses which follow should demonstrate, is consistent with Eagleton's "discourse analysis," or "rhetoric."

28. Fredric Jameson, *The Political Unconscious: Narrative as a Socially Symbolic Act* (Ithaca, N.Y., 1981), p. 107; hereafter cited in text as *TPU*.

29. Leslie Fiedler, "Literature as an Institution: the View from 1980," in Leslie Fiedler and Houston Baker, Jr., eds., *English Literature: Opening Up the Canon: Selected Papers from the English Institute, 1979* (Baltimore, 1981), p. 73.

30. Roland Barthes, "Reflexions sur un Manuel," in Serge Doubrovski and Tzvetan Todorov, eds., *L'Enseignement de la Littérature* (Paris, 1971), p. 170, my translation.

31. Raymond Williams, *Marxism and Literature*, p. 116.

32. Antonio Gramsci, quoted by Evan Watkins in "Conflict and Consensus in the History of Recent Criticism," *New Literary History* 12 (Winter 1981):359.

33. Fredric Jameson, "Marxism and Historicism," p. 57.

2 / Indian Autobiography: Origins, Type, and Function

1. James M. Cox, "Autobiography and America," in *Aspects of Narrative: Selected Papers from the English Institute*, ed. J. Hillis Miller (New York, 1971), p. 145.

2. George and Louise Spindler, "American Indian Personality Types and Their Sociocultural Roots," quoted by Harold E. Driver, *Indians of North America*, 2d ed., rev. (Chicago, 1975), p. 434.

3. Tzvetan Todorov, *The Fantastic: A Structural Approach to a Literary Genre*, trans. Richard Howard (Ithaca, N.Y., 1975), p. 3.

4. James Axtell, "The Ethnohistory of Early America: A Review Essay," *The William and Mary Quarterly* 35 (Jan. 1978):116.

Notes

5. Edward Said, "The Problem of Textuality: Two Exemplary Positions," *Critical Inquiry* 4 (1978):675, and 709n.

6. See Francis Jennings, *The Invasion of America: Indians, Colonialism, and the Cant of Conquest* (New York, 1976).

7. See Roy Harvey Pearce, *Savagism and Civilization* (Baltimore, 1967), originally published in 1953 as *The Savages of America: A Study of the Indian and the Idea of Civilization*, chap. 4, "The Zero of Human Society: The Idea of the Savage."

8. Ambrose Bierce, *The Devil's Dictionary* (New York, 1958), p. 7. Bierce wrote his definitions between 1881 and 1906.

9. Quoted by Marjorie Halpin in her introduction to Catlin's *Letters and Notes on the Manners, Customs, and Conditions of North American Indians* (New York, 1973), I:ix. Catlin's work was first published in London in 1841.

10. A. D. Coleman in an introduction to Edward S. Curtis, *Portraits from North American Indian Life* (n.p., 1972), p. v. Curtis's work was originally published in a limited edition of five hundred sets (priced at $3,000 each) in 1907–1908.

11. William Fenton in his introduction to B. B. Thatcher's *Indian Biography* (Glorieta, N.M., 1973), unpaged. This is a reprint of the New York edition of 1832; an edition appeared in Boston in the same year.

12. Thatcher, *Indian Biography*, unpaged. Further quotations from Thatcher are taken from this preface.

13. See Richard Slotkin, *Regeneration Through Violence: The Mythology of the American Frontier, 1600–1860* (Middletown, Conn., 1974), especially chaps. 9 and 10.

14. Louis O. Mink, "Narrative Form as a Cognitive Instrument," in *The Writing of History: Literary Form and Historical Understanding*, eds. R. H. Canary and Henry Kozicki (Madison, 1978), p. 138.

15. Quoted in John Bakeless, *Daniel Boone: Master of the Wilderness* (New York, 1939), passim.

16. David Crockett, in the preface to his *A Narrative of the Life of David Crockett of the State of Tennessee, Written by Himself*, ed. Joseph J. Arpad (New Haven, 1972), p. 47. Crockett's *Narrative* was originally published in Philadelphia in 1834.

17. Louis P. Renza, "The Veto of the Imagination: A Theory of

Notes

Autobiography," *New Literary History* 9 (1977):2. Renza's sentence concludes, autobiography "is definable as a form of 'prose fiction.'"

18. Ibid.

19. Crockett, *A Narrative*, pp. 47–48.

20. In his introduction to *Kit Carson's Autobiography*, edited by Quaife (Chicago, 1935; rpt. Lincoln, Nebr., n.d.), pp. xvii–xxviii. The *Autobiography* was originally published in late 1858 or early 1859 in New York.

21. See the *Life of Sam Houston of Texas* (New York, 1855), unsigned, by Charles Edward Lester, under Houston's supervision; also the *Life of General Sam Houston: A Short Autobiography* (Austin, Tex., 1964), originally published in 1855; and T. D. Bonner, *The Life and Adventures of James P. Beckwourth* (New York, 1969), originally published in New York in 1856.

22. William T. Hagan, *American Indians*, rev. ed. (Chicago, 1979), p. 72.

23. Translator's preface to *Black Hawk: An Autobiography*, ed. Donald Jackson (Urbana, 1964), unpaged. The full title of the original 1833 edition published at Cincinnati is the *Life of Ma-Ka-Tai-Me-She-Kia-Kiak or Black Hawk, embracing the Tradition of his Nation—Indian Wars in which he has been engaged—Cause of joining the British in their late War with America, and its History—Description of the Rock-River Village—Manners and Customs—Encroachments by the Whites, Contrary to Treaty—Removal from his Village in 1831. With an Account of the Cause and General History of the Late War, his Surrender and Confinement at Jefferson Barracks, and Travels through the United States. Dictated by Himself.* All quotations are from Jackson's edition in which the translator's preface, Black Hawk's dedication, and the editor's "Advertisement" are unpaged. Page references will be given in the text.

24. Quoted by Donald Jackson in his introduction to *Black Hawk: An Autobiography*, p. 28.

25. Ibid., p. 26.

26. Thatcher, preface to *Indian Biography*, unpaged.

27. Slotkin, *Regeneration Through Violence*, p. 426.

28. John Filson, *The Discovery, Settlement and Present State of Kentucke*, which includes as an appendix "The Adventures of Col. Daniel

Notes

Boon, one of the first settlers, containing a 'Narrative of the Wars of Kentucke'" (Gloucester, Mass., 1975), pp. 81–82. Filson's book was originally published in Wilmington, Delaware, in 1784.

29. *Emplotment* is Hayden White's term for the large structures Frye would probably call "myths," as they appear in the narratives of "history." See Hayden White, *Metahistory: The Historical Imagination in Nineteenth-Century Europe* (Baltimore, 1973), and "The Historical Text as Literary Artifact," in *The Writing of History*, eds. Canary and Kozicki. The quotations from Frye are from the *Anatomy of Criticism* (New York, 1965), pp. 169ff.

30. Benjamin F. Drake, *The Life and Adventures of Black Hawk* (Cincinnati, 1838), pp. 20–21.

31. From the title page of the first edition, Boston, 1832.

32. Two editions in Boston in 1834; one in Philadelphia in 1834, together with an account of "a Lady who was taken prisoner by the Indians"; and one in New York in 1834. Other editions: London, 1836; Cooperstown, 1842; Boston, 1845; Leeuwarden, Netherlands, 1847—this is listed in Sabin, *Bibliotheca Americana: Dictionary of Books Relating to America from its Discovery to the Present Time* (New York, 1868; rpt. New York, n.d.) under LeClair's pseudonym, "R. Postumus"; Cincinnati, 1858; St. Louis, 1882; Chicago, 1916; and Iowa City, 1932.

3 / History, Science, and Geronimo's Story

1. In Florida, however, the Seminole continued to resist American aggression, at least until the death of Osceola in 1838.

2. Henry Nash Smith, *Virgin Land: The American West as Symbol and Myth* (Cambridge, Mass., 1950), pp. 123–132.

3. Hagan, *American Indians*, p. 112.

4. Chief Joseph White Bull, allegedly "the warrior who killed Custer," was prevailed upon to write the story of his life in 1931, more than a half century after the Custer battle. White Bull, like his uncle Sitting Bull (q.v.), also drew pictorial representations of his coups. See James H. Howard, trans. and ed., *The Warrior Who Killed Custer* (Lincoln, Nebr., 1968) and, for an account that includes White Bull's comments in a 1932 interview, Stanley Vestal, "The Man Who Killed Custer,"

American Heritage 8 (1957):4–9, 90–91, and also Vestal's *Warpath: The True Story of the Fighting Sioux, Told in a Biography of Chief White Bull* (Boston, 1934).

5. Quoted in Virginia I. Armstrong, ed., *I Have Spoken: American History through the Voices of the Indians* (New York, 1972), p. 146.

6. Lynne Woods O'Brien, *Plains Indian Autobiographies* (Boise, 1973), p. 12.

7. Ibid.

8. Ibid., pp. 12–13.

9. Quoted as an "oversimplification" by Merrill D. Beal in the preface to his *"I Will Fight No More Forever": Chief Joseph and the Nez Perce War* (New York, 1971), p. xv.

10. Francis Paul Prucha, S.J., ed., *Americanizing the American Indians: Writings by the "Friends of the Indian," 1880–1900* (Cambridge, Mass., 1973), p. 6.

11. Hagan, *American Indians*, p. 141.

12. S. M. Barrett, ed., "Introductory" to *Geronimo's Story of His Life* (Williamstown, Mass., 1973), p. xiii. This is a reprint of the original edition published in New York by Duffield and Co. in 1906. Further references are to this edition and will be documented in the text.

13. *Geronimo: His Own Story*, edited by S. M. Barrett, newly edited with introduction and notes by Frederick W. Turner III (New York, 1971), p. 46.

14. Turner writes, "The materials related to the surrender of Geronimo and the Chiricahua originally followed Chapter xvi but more properly belong in an appendix" (p. 185). This is mistaken on two counts: first, the materials belong "properly" wherever Barrett put them; additional interpretive adjustments only move us further from historical accuracy. Second, "These materials" originally followed chapter xvii, not chapter xvi; they appear in chapter xviii of the original.

15. Henry David Thoreau, *Walden and Civil Disobedience* (New York, 1966), p. 1.

16. Edward B. Tylor, *Primitive Culture*, quoted in A. L. Kroeber and Clyde Kluckhohn, *Culture: a Critical review of concepts and definitions* (New York, 1953), p. 81. Kroeber and Kluckhohn give the edition

Notes

as Boston, 1871. The first edition of Tylor's important work was published by J. Murray in London in 1871, and the National Union Catalog indicates the first American edition to be Boston (Estes and Luriat) and New York (Henry Holt), 1874. I have found no reference to a Boston edition of 1871. I may have overlooked something of course, but if not, this seems worth mentioning in specific relation to the rather widespread disregard by anthropologists for such things as the original dates and places of publication of books, as if these were not potentially useful bits of information. Kroeber and Kluckhohn note that ". . . American anthropologists were using both the concept and the word culture fairly freely in the eighteen-nineties, perhaps already in the eighties . . ." (p. 296), but that they do not define it until the 1920s—and that this may well be a result of Boas's (q.v.) antitheoretical stance.

17. Quoted by Perry Miller, "The Marrow of Puritan Divinity," in *Errand Into the Wilderness* (Cambridge, Mass., 1956), p. 60.

18. The best general account of these matters and of the terms I have enclosed within quotation marks is Harris's *The Rise of Anthropological Theory.*

19. Hayden White, *Metahistory*, passim. White's characterization of ironic historiography in *Metahistory* notes that it marks an ending, serving to "undermine confidence in history's claim to 'objectivity,' 'scienticity,' and 'realism'" (p. 41). But the ironic mode in anthropology coincides with a pronounced sense of beginning and thus more nearly defines rather than undermines a particular *kind* of commitment to "objectivity," "scienticity," and "realism." All of *Metahistory* can stand as a critique of the "fact"/"interpretation" opposition.

20. Alfred Kroeber's Gros Ventre war narratives, obtained in 1901 (in *Ethnology of the Gros Ventre*, Anthropological Papers, American Museum of Natural History, vol. 1, part 4, 1908), as an attempt to "give a truer sample of the nature of the *average* Gros Ventre war exploit, of the *average* war participation, and the like . . ." [Alfred Kroeber, "A Yurok War Reminiscence: The Use of Autobiographical Evidence," *Southwestern Journal of Anthropology* I (1945):318–332, quotation from pp. 321–322, my emphasis], may, strictly speaking, have been the first "professional" writing of "life history," or Indian autobiography. Radin's were by far the more influential.

21. Jackson, introduction to *Black Hawk*, p. 27.

22. That Barrett could write about Indians differently—for better or for worse—is suggested by the following passages from his *Mocco, An Indian Boy* (New York, 1911):

> He seated himself where his enemy had been lying in wait for him and pondered long. He could form no definite plan, but mechanically he turned toward home, or at least toward where home had been. It was a long fifteen miles he had come, and it seemed longer when without purpose or hope he turned, weak from hunger, worn from loss of sleep, and exhausted by prolonged excitement, back to the old camp.
>
> At the camp he was leaving were fragments of food he would fain have eaten, but they were the leavings of his enemies, and he spurned to eat what was cast away by the Comanches. (Pp. 98–99)

Mocco is baptized; finally, he dies of yellow fever. The book ends:

> In spite of this illness Mocco rode on, but the heat of the sun and absence of water rendered him unable to ride far. Soon he was lying delirious on the plains. A rain in the afternoon drenched him and cooled his fever so that consciousness was restored. He called his horse to him but was unable to mount. On the next day he became delirious again, and in his delirium often spoke Fawn's name.
>
> That night he feebly placed his hands to his mouth and gave the lion's call four times. As he waited, listening for the answer, he came to the end of the "Long Trail," and his soul passed on into spirit land to be judged by a merciful Father.
>
> A few years later some Pawnee Indians captured a fine black horse on their hunting grounds. Near where they first saw him they found a rusty rifle, a curious dagger, and a little black cross lying among scattered bones. (Pp. 190–191)

The frontispiece to the book is a photograph of Fawn. Whether this text is based on historical material or is purely invented, whether it is intended for an adult or a juvenile audience, I have been unable to discover.

23. Frye, *Anatomy of Criticism*, p. 167.

24. See James Kaywaykla, *In the Days of Victorio, Recollections of a Warm Springs Apache*, ed. Eve Ball (Tucson, 1970); Samuel Kenoi,

---

"A Chiricahua's Account of the Geronimo Campaign of 1886," ed. Morris Opler, *New Mexico Historical Review* 13 (1938):360–386; and Jason Betzinez, *I Fought with Geronimo*, with Wilber S. Nye (New York, 1959).

25. Fredric Jameson, "Marxism and Historicism," p. 69.

4 / The Case of Crashing Thunder

1. The major attack on Boas remains that of Leslie White in *The Ethnography and Ethnology of Franz Boas*, Austin Texas Memorial Museum, The Museum of the University of Texas, bulletin no. 6, 1963. Marvin Harris, in *The Rise of Anthropological Theory*, is also quite critical. The comments of Boas's first students, over the years and in a variety of contexts, are too diverse to characterize simply as positive or negative, although in the main they are overwhelmingly praising of the man and his work. Boas's reputation continues to inspire interest. See for example a defense of his ethnography by one of his last students, Irving Goldman, "Boas on the Kwakiutl: The Ethnographic Tradition," in *Theory and Practice: Essays Presented to Gene Weltfish*, ed. Stanley Diamond (The Hague, 1979), and Karl Kroeber's comments in his exchange with David Brumble, in "Reasoning Together," *The Canadian Review of American Studies* 11 (1981):253–270.

2. Goody, *Domestication of the Savage Mind*, pp. 147–162ff.

3. Marvin Harris, *Rise of Anthropological Theory*, p. 282.

4. Ibid.

5. Marvin Harris, *Rise of Anthropological Theory*, p. 316.

6. Marvin Harris, *Cultural Materialism*, p. 316.

7. Paul Radin, preface to "The Personal Reminiscences of a Winnebago Indian," *Journal of American Folklore* 26 (1913):293; hereafter cited in text as *PR*.

8. Franz Boas, "Recent Anthropology II," *Science* 98 (1943):335.

9. Paul Radin, preface to *The Winnebago Tribe*, Thirty-Seventh Annual Report of the Bureau of American Ethnology, 1915–1916 (Washington, 1923), p. 47; hereafter cited in text as *WT*.

10. Paul Radin, introduction to *The Autobiography of a Winnebago Indian* (New York, 1963), p. 2; hereafter cited in text as *A*. Original

publication of the *Autobiography*, as noted, was in the *University of California Publications in American Archaeology and Ethnology* 16 (April 15, 1920):381–473.

11. Elsie Clews Parsons, preface to *American Indian Life* (Lincoln, Nebr., 1967), p. 2. Original publication was in 1922.

12. A. L. Kroeber, introduction to Parsons, *American Indian Life*, p. 13.

13. For the real subjects of these anthropologists' fictions, see H. David Brumble, *An Annotated Bibliography of American Indian and Eskimo Autobiographies* (Lincoln, Nebr., 1981), #462.

14. In his introduction to *The Road of Life and Death: A Ritual Drama of the American Indian* (New York, 1945), Radin tells of pursuing the reluctant Jasper Blowsnake with a horse and wagon (pp. 44ff); hereafter cited in text as *RLD*. Later, Radin visited Nancy O. Lurie and Mountain Wolf Woman when they were at work on the latter's autobiography in 1958. According to Lurie, " . . . Paul Radin questioned [Mountain Wolf Woman] about peyote before we reached this point in her account. Since he spoke of her brother's first vision in what she considered an offhand manner, she did not want to speak of a matter of such deep emotional significance to herself. Dr. Radin expressed mild amusement that her brother's first vision had included frightening snakes, so she confined herself to telling him a funny incident in regard to an early peyote experience," Nancy O. Lurie, ed., *Mountain Wolf Woman: Sister of Crashing Thunder, the Autobiography of a Winnebago Indian* (Ann Arbor, 1961), p. 127. All further references to this work, abbreviated *MWW*, will be included in the text. Working some thirty years after Radin, Lurie was herself particularly sensitive to and aware of the complexities of "influence." Radin's own sensitivity to this issue, such as it may have been, seems fairly illustrated by some remarks he made only a year after the publication of *Crashing Thunder*. In his preface to *Primitive Man as Philosopher* (New York, 1927), he acknowledged that, for all their commitment to objectivity, " . . . ethnologists often find it necessary to give what are simply their own impressions and interpretations." But this seemed to him not fit subject for concern, for, as he continued, "I must confess myself to have had frequent recourse to impressions and interpretations, which I have then sought to illustrate by appropriate examples.

Notes

But I realize quite clearly *how easy it is to obtain appropriate examples,* and mine, I hope, have been chosen judiciously" (p. xi, my emphasis).

15. Paul Radin's introduction to *Crashing Thunder: The Autobiography of an American Indian* (New York, 1926), p. xi; hereafter cited in text as *CT.*

16. Nancy Lurie's comments on these matters are particularly valuable. According to Lurie:

> . . . Radin was inspired to try to capture more of the eloquence of the Winnebago text in the "liberties" he took with the translation as received from La Mere. Gazing probably comes closer than looking, e.g. The "would I", in the example you [A.K.] give, might be a better choice than "I would." Pronouns are all bound forms, infixed into the verb and even the word "sit" in the first version is a bound form of the verb, in effect gazing-while-sitting, all one verb with the pronoun and mood also infixed. At this time, of course, it would be hard to say whether Radin was being more "literary" in somewhat outmoded Euramerican terms or more "literary" in trying to convey the Winnebago delight in speech as an art. . . . "it is said" is probably closer to the Winnebago original than "I have been told." The sentence in Winnebago probably was boy, good tempered, I was, it is said. Even that doesn't do it literally because of the pronouns. (Personal communication)

17. Ruth Underhill, foreword to Lurie's *Mountain Wolf Woman,* p. ix.

18. L. L. Langness, *The Life History in Anthropological Science* (New York, 1965), p. 7, and L. L. Langness and Gelya Frank, *Lives: An Anthropological Approach to Biography* (Novato, Calif., 1981), p. 18. Just how "rigorous" Radin actually was we shall soon examine.

19. George E. Marcus and Dick Cushman, "Ethnographies as Texts," *Annual Review of Anthropology* 11 (1982):56n.

20. Underhill, *Mountain Wolf Woman,* p. ix.

21. Brumble, "Reasoning Together," p. 269.

22. Underhill, *Mountain Wolf Woman,* p. ix.

Notes

5 / Yellow Wolf and Black Elk: History and Transcendence

1. Marvin Harris, *The Rise of Anthropological Theory*, p. 422.

2. Claude Lévi-Strauss, review of Leo Simmons's *Sun Chief, The Autobiography of a Hopi Indian*, in *Social Research* 10 (1943):516.

3. Ibid.

4. Leo W. Simmons, *Sun Chief, The Autobiography of a Hopi Indian* (New Haven, 1942), p. 401.

5. In "The Use of Personal Documents in History, Anthropology, and Sociology," *Social Science Research Bulletin*, no. 53 (1945):77–173.

6. Franz Boas, "Recent Anthropology II," *Science* 98 (October 15, 1943):335.

7. Marvin Harris, *The Rise of Anthropological Theory*, p. 393.

8. This is not at all to say these warriors would readily have provided such information or understood how it might seem important. But the anthropologists of the day were quite adept at overcoming initial Native reluctance; had they so desired, they might well have elicited this sort of material.

9. H. David Brumble, "Sam Blowsnake's Invention of Autobiography: *Crashing Thunder* and the History of American Indian Autobiography," paper presented at the Modern Language Association Convention, December 1983.

10. Clyde Kluckhohn, "The Personal Document in Anthropological Science," in *The Use of Personal Documents in History, Anthropology, and Sociology*, p. 91.

11. Gilbert Wilson, ed., *Goodbird the Indian* (New York, 1914), pp. 79–80.

12. Simmons, *Sun Chief*, p. 381.

13. Ibid.

14. Inasmuch as the salvage anthropologists were committed to the ongoing existence of the Indian, one can understand easily enough why tragic stories of decline and fall or of defeat and death were not attractive to them. The comic mode is most readily applicable to a preservationist perspective, whereas the ironic at least permits continuation—if to no particular point.

Notes

15. Lucullus Virgil McWhorter, *Yellow Wolf: His Own Story* (Caldwell, Idaho, 1940), unpaged. Further references will be documented in the text.

16. See Kluckhohn, chap. 3, "Field Techniques and Methods," in *Use of Personal Documents*, pp. 109–132.

17. McWhorter's procedure had to some extent been anticipated by Frank Bird Linderman in his biographies or, perhaps, they are autobiographies of Plenty-Coups [*American: The Life Story of a Great Indian* (New York, 1930); rpt. *Plenty-Coups, Chief of the Crows* (Lincoln, Nebr., 1962)] and Pretty Shield [*Red Mother* (New York, 1932); rpt. *Pretty-Shield: Medicine Woman of the Crows* (Lincoln, Nebr., 1974)].

18. See F. H. Matthews, "The Revolt against Americanism: Cultural Pluralism and Cultural Relativism as an Ideology of Liberation," *Canadian Review of American Studies* (Spring 1970):4–31.

19. Neither Kluckhohn in his survey of "personal documents" in anthropology, nor Louis Gottschalk in his "The Historian and the Historical Document" in the same volume, refers to McWhorter or to Yellow Wolf, however.

20. *Hear Me, My Chiefs: Nez Perce History and Legend*, ed. Ruth Bordin (Caldwell, Idaho, 1952), p. 2. This volume also contains an extended autobiographical narrative of the Nez Perce, Two Moons.

21. Frye, *Anatomy of Criticism*, p. 208.

22. Cyrus Townsend Brady, *Northwestern Fights and Fighters* (New York, 1907; rpt. Williamstown, Mass., 1974). Brady's book is dedicated to "the peace loving, hard working, honor seeking, duty following, never failing, hard fighting ARMY OF THE UNITED STATES."

23. See Nelson A. Miles, *Personal Recollections* (Chicago, 1897); O. O. Howard, *Nez Perce Joseph* (Boston, 1881) and *My Life and Experiences Among our Hostile Indians* (Hartford, 1907).

24. Mary Austin, "The Path on the Rainbow," *Dial* 31 (May, 1919):569.

25. See Robert F. Sayre, "Vision and Experience in *Black Elk Speaks*," *College English* 32 (February, 1971):509–535; Sally McCluskey, "Black Elk Speaks: And So Does John Neihardt," *Western American Literature* 6 (1972):231–242; Michael Castro, "John G. Neihardt," in *Interpreting the Indian: Twentieth Century Poets and the Native Amer-*

ican (Albuquerque, 1983), pp. 79–99; Clyde Holler, "Lakota Religion and Tragedy: The Theology of *Black Elk Speaks*," *Journal of the American Academy of Religion*, forthcoming.

26. *Black Elk Speaks*, ed. John G. Neihardt, with an introduction by Vine Deloria (Lincoln, Nebr., 1979), p. 270. This University of Nebraska Press edition, to which I shall refer, documenting further page references in the text, is a reprint of the original 1932 edition.

27. Quoted by Sally McCluskey, "Black Elk Speaks," pp. 238–239.

28. Clyde Holler, "Lakota Religion and Tragedy," p. 39. All further references to this work will be documented in the text.

29. See Lucille F. Aly, "Poetry and History in Neihardt's *Cycle of the West*," *Western American Literature* 16 (Spring 1981):3–18; and David C. Young, "Crazy Horse on the Trojan Plain: A Comment on the Classicism of John G. Neihardt," *Classical and Modern Literature* 3 (1982):45–53.

30. Inasmuch as the modes of emplotment are culturally determined they are not therefore susceptible of subversion by the practice of a single author or the example of a single text. Indeed, any apparently open-ended, unemplotted narrative—Kafka's *The Castle*, for example—does not evade structural typing but, rather, becomes inevitably an example of ironic emplotment.

31. Michael Castro, *Interpreting the Indian*, p. 86, my emphasis.

32. Ibid., p. 89.

33. Frye, *Anatomy of Criticism*, p. 187.

34. Ibid.

35. Ibid., p. 33.

36. There is no date given for Deloria's introduction although the flap copy refers to it as an Introduction to "this special edition." Deloria himself is obviously more interested in eternity than time.

37. Frye, *Anatomy of Criticism*, p. 186.

38. See Thomas E. Mails, *Fools Crow* (Garden City, N.Y., 1979); Richard Erdoes and John (Fire) Lame Deer, *Lame Deer: Seeker of Visions* (New York, 1972); Charlotte J. Frisbie and David P. McAllester, *Navajo Blessingway Singer: The Autobiography of Frank Mitchell, 1881–1967* (Tucson, 1978).

Selected Bibliography

Aly, Lucille F. "Poetry and History in Neihardt's *Cycle of the West*," *Western American Literature* 16 (Spring 1981): 3–18.

Armstrong, Virginia I., ed. *I have Spoken: American History through the Voices of the Indians*. New York: Pocket Books, 1972.

Austin, Mary. *The American Rhythm: Studies and Reëxpressions of Amerindian Songs*. Boston: Houghton Miflin, 1923; reprint ed., New York: Folcroft, 1980.

———. "The Path on the Rainbow," *Dial* 31 (May 1919): 569–570.

Axtell, James. "The Ethnohistory of Early America: A Review Essay," *The William and Mary Quarterly* 35 (January 1978): 110–144.

Bakeless, John. *Daniel Boone: Master of the Wilderness*. New York: William Morrow, 1939.

Barrett, S. M., ed. *Geronimo's Story of His Life* (New York: Duffield and Co., 1906).

———. *Mocco, An Indian Boy*. New York: Duffield and Co., 1911.

Barthes, Roland. "Reflexions Sur Un Manuel." *In* Serge Doubrovski and Tzvetan Todorov, eds. *L'Enseignement de la littérature*. Paris: Plon, 1971. Pp. 170–177.

Beal, Merrill D. *"I Will Fight No More Forever": Chief Joseph and the Nez Perce War*. New York: Ballantine Books, 1971.

Betzinez, Jason. *I Fought With Geronimo*. With Wilber S. Nye. New York: Bonanza Books, 1959.

Bevis, William. "American Indian Verse Translations," *College English* 35 (March 1974): 693–703.

Bierce, Ambrose. *The Devil's Dictionary*. New York: Dover, 1958.

Bierhorst, John, ed. *In the Trail of the Wind: American Indian Poems and Ritual Orations*. New York: Farrar, Straus and Giroux, 1971.

Boas, Franz. "Recent Anthropology II," *Science* 98 (October 15, 1943): 334–337.

Bonner, T. D. *The Life and Adventures of James P. Beckwourth.* New York, 1856; reprint ed., New York: Ayer, 1969.

Bordin, Ruth, ed. *Hear Me, My Chiefs: Nez Perce History and Legend.* Caldwell, Idaho: Caxton Printers, 1952.

Brady, Cyrus Townsend, ed. *Northwestern Fights and Fighters.* New York: McClure Co., 1907; reprint ed., Williamstown, Mass.: Corner House Publishers, 1974.

Brandon, William, ed. *The Magic World: American Indian Songs and Poems.* New York: William Morrow, 1971.

Brumble, H. David, III. *An Annotated Bibliography of American Indian and Eskimo Autobiographies.* Lincoln: University of Nebraska Press, 1981.

————— . "Sam Blowsnake's Invention of Autobiography: *Crashing Thunder* and the History of American Indian Autobiography," paper presented at the 100th meeting of the Modern Language Association, New York, N.Y., 27 December 1983.

Brumble, H. David, III, and Kroeber, Karl. "Reasoning Together," *Canadian Review of American Studies* 11 (1981): 253–270.

Castro, Michael. *Interpreting the Indian.* Albuquerque: University of New Mexico Press, 1983.

Catlin, George. *Letters and Notes on the Manners, Customs, and Conditions of North American Indians.* London, 1841; reprint ed., New York, Dover, 1973.

Charvat, William. *The Profession of Authorship in America, 1800–1870.* Columbus: Ohio State University Press, 1968.

Clements, William M. "Faking the Pumpkin: On Jerome Rothenberg's Literary Offenses," *Western American Literature* 16 (November 1981): 193–204.

Coleman, A. D. Introduction to E. S. Curtis, *Portraits from North American Indian Life.* N.p.: A. and W. Visual Library, 1972.

Cox, James M. "Autobiography and America." *In* J. Hillis Miller, ed. *Aspects of Narrative: Selected Papers from the English Institute.* New York: Columbia University Press, 1971. Pp. 143–172.

Crockett, David. *A Narrative of the Life of David Crockett of the State of Tennessee, Written by Himself.* Edited by Joseph J. Arpad. New Haven: College and University Press, 1972.

[154]

Selected Bibliography

Deloria, Vine, Jr. Introduction to John G. Neihardt, ed., *Black Elk Speaks*. Lincoln: University of Nebraska Press, 1979.

De Man, Paul. "The Epistemology of Metaphor," *Critical Inquiry* 5 (Autumn 1978): 13–30.

Dollard, John. *Criteria for the Life History*. New Haven: Yale University Press, 1935.

Drake, Benjamin F. *The Life and Adventures of Black Hawk*. Cincinnati, 1838.

Driver, Harold E. *Indians of North America*. 2d ed., rev. Chicago: University of Chicago Press, 1975.

Dyk, Walter, ed. *Son of Old Man Hat: A Navaho Autobiography*. New York: Harcourt, Brace, 1938; reprint ed., Lincoln: University of Nebraska Press, 1967.

Dyk, Walter, and Dyk, Ruth, eds. *Left-Handed: A Navajo Autobiography*. New York: Columbia University Press, 1980.

Eagleton, Terry. *Literary Theory: An Introduction*. Minneapolis: University of Minnesota Press, 1983.

Erdoes, Richard, and Lame Deer, John (Fire). *Lame Deer: Seeker of Visions*. New York: Simon and Schuster, 1972.

Fenton, William. Introduction to B. B. Thatcher, *Indian Biography*. Glorieta, N.M.: Rio Grande Press, 1973.

Fielder, Leslie. "Literature as an Institution: the View from 1980." *In* Leslie Fiedler and Houston Baker, Jr., eds., *English Literature: Opening Up the Canon, Selected Papers from the English Institute, 1979*. Baltimore: Johns Hopkins University Press, 1981. Pp. 78–91.

Filson, John. *The Discovery, Settlement, and Present State of Kentucke*. Wilmington, Del., 1784; reprint ed., Gloucester, Mass.: Peter Smith, 1975.

Foucault, Michel. "What Is an Author?" *In* Donald F. Bouchard, ed., *Language, Counter-Memory, Practice: Selected Essays and Interviews*. Ithaca, N.Y.: Cornell University Press, 1977. Pp. 113–138.

Freeman, John F. *A Guide to Manuscripts Relating to the American Indian in the Library of the American Philosophical Library*. Philadelphia: American Philosophical Society, 1966.

Frisbie, Charlotte J., and McAllester, David P., eds. *Navajo Blessingway*

Singer: The Autobiography of Frank Mitchell, 1881–1967. Tucson: University of Arizona Press, 1978.

Frye, Northrop. *Anatomy of Criticism*. New York: Atheneum, 1965.

Geronimo. *Geronimo's Story of His Life*. Edited by S. M. Barrett. New York: Duffield and Co., 1906; reprint ed., Williamstown, Mass.: Corner House Publishers, 1973.

Goldman, Irving. "Boas on the Kwakiutl: The Ethnographic Tradition." *In* Stanley Diamond, ed., *Theory and Practice: Essays Presented to Gene Weltfish*. The Hague: Mouton, 1979. Pp. 331–345.

Goody, Jack. *The Domestication of the Savage Mind*. Cambridge: Cambridge University Press, 1977.

Hagan, William T. *American Indians*. Rev. ed. Chicago: University of Chicago Press, 1979.

Halpin, Marjorie. Introduction to George Catlin, *Letters and Notes on the Manners, Customs, and Conditions of North American Indians*. Vol. 1. New York: Dover, 1973.

Harris, Marvin. *Cultural Materialism: The Struggle for a Science of Culture*. New York: Vintage Books, 1979.

——— . *The Rise of Anthropological Theory*. New York: Harper and Row, 1979.

Holler, Clyde C. "Lakota Religion and Tragedy: The Theology of Black Elk Speaks," *Journal of the American Academy of Religion*, in press.

Howard, James H., trans. and ed. *The Warrior Who Killed Custer*. Lincoln: University of Nebraska Press, 1968.

Howard, O. O. *My Life and Experiences Among Our Hostile Indians*. Hartford: A. D. Worthington, 1907.

——— . *Nez Perce Joseph*. Boston, 1881.

Hymes, Dell. "Breakthrough Into Performance." *In* Dan Ben-Amos and Kenneth S. Goldstein, eds., *Folklore: Performance and Communication*. The Hague: Mouton, 1975. Pp. 11–74.

——— . "Discovering Oral Performance and Measured Verse in American Indian Narrative," *New Literary History* 8 (Spring 1977): 431–457.

——— . *In Vain I Tried To Tell You: Essays in Native American Ethnopoetics*. Philadelphia: University of Pennsylvania Press, 1981.

——— . "Reading Clackamas Texts." *In* Karl Kroeber, ed., *Traditional*

Native American Literatures. Lincoln: University of Nebraska Press, 1981. Pp. 117–159.

_____ . "Some North Pacific Coast Poems: A Problem in Anthropological Philology," *American Anthropologist* 67 (1965): 316–341.

Jackson, Donald, ed. *Black Hawk: An Autobiography*. Urbana: University of Illinois Press, 1964.

Jameson, Fredric. "Marxism and Historicism," *New Literary History* 11 (Autumn 1979): 41–73.

_____ . *The Political Unconscious: Narrative as a Socially Symbolic Act*. Ithaca: Cornell University Press, 1981.

Jennings, Francis. *The Invasion of America: Indians, Colonialism, and the Cant of Conquest*. New York: W. W. Norton, 1976.

Kaywaykla, James. *In The Days of Victorio, Recollections of a Warm Springs Apache*. Edited by Eve Ball. Tucson: University of Arizona Press, 1970.

Kenoi, Samuel. "A Chiricahua's Account of the Geronimo Campaign of 1886." Edited by Morris Opler. *New Mexico Historical Review* 13 (1938): 360–386.

Kermode, Frank. *The Genesis of Secrecy: On the Interpretation of Narrative*. Cambridge, Mass.: Harvard University Press, 1979.

Kluckhohn, Clyde. "The Personal Document in Anthropological Science." *In* Robert Angell, Louis Gottschalk, and Clyde Kluckhohn, *The Use of Personal Documents in History, Anthropology, and Sociology*, Social Science Research Bulletin, no. 53, New York, 1945. Pp. 77–173.

Kroeber, Alfred. *Ethnology of the Gros Ventre*. Anthropological Papers, American Museum of Natural History, vol. 1, part 4, New York, 1908.

_____ . "A Yurok War Reminiscence: The Use of Autobiographical Evidence," *Southwestern Journal of Anthropology* 1 (1945): 318–332.

Langness, L. L. *The Life History in Anthropological Science*. New York: Holt, Rinehart and Winston, 1965.

Langness, L. L., and Frank, Gelya. *Lives: An Anthropological Approach to Biography*. Novato, Calif.: Chandler and Sharp, 1981.

Lester, Charles Edward. *Life of Sam Houston of Texas*, New York, 1855.

Selected Bibliography

———. *The Life of General Sam Houston: A Short Autobiography*. N.p., 1855; reprint ed., Austin, Texas: The Pemberton Press, 1964.

Lévi-Straus, Claude. Review of Leo Simmons, *Sun Chief: The Autobiography of A Hopi Indian*. *Social Research* 10 (1943): 515–517.

Liberty, Margot. "Francis La Flesche: The Osage Odyssey." *In* Margot Liberty, ed., *American Indian Intellectuals*. St. Paul, Minn.: West Publishing Co., 1978. Pp. 45–59.

Linderman, Frank Bird. *American: The Life Story of a Great Indian*. New York: The John Day Co., 1930; reprint ed., *Plenty-Coups, Chief of the Crows*. Lincoln: University of Nebraska Press, 1962.

———. *Red Mother*. New York: The John Day Co., 1932; reprint ed., *Pretty Shield: Medicine Woman of the Crows*. Lincoln: University of Nebraska Press, 1974.

Lurie, Nancy O. Notes to Nancy O. Lurie, ed., *Mountain Wolf Woman: Sister of Crashing Thunder*. Ann Arbor: University of Michigan Press, 1961.

Macherey, Pierre. *A Theory of Literary Production*. London: Routledge and Kegan Paul, 1978.

Mails, Thomas E., ed. *Fools Crow*. Garden City, N.Y.: Doubleday and Co., 1979.

Marcus, George E., and Cushman, Dick. "Ethnographies as Texts," *Annual Review of Anthropology* 11 (1982): 25–69.

Matthews, F. H. "The Revolt Against Americanism: Cultural Pluralism and Cultural Relativism as an Ideology of Liberation," *Canadian Review of American Studies* 1 (Spring 1970): 4–31.

McCluskey, Sally. "Black Elk Speaks: And So Does John Neihardt," *Western American Literature* 6 (1972): 231–242.

McWhorter, Lucullus Virgil. *Hear Me, My Chiefs: Nez Perce History and Legend*. Edited by Ruth Bordin. Caldwell, Idaho: Caxton Printers, 1952.

———. *Yellow Wolf: His Own Story*. Caldwell, Idaho: Caxton Printers, 1940.

Miles, Nelson A. *Personal Recollections*. Chicago, 1897.

Miller, Perry. *Errand Into the Wilderness*. Cambridge, Mass.: Harvard University Press, 1956.

Mink, Louis O. "Narrative Form as a Cognitive Instrument." *In* R. H. Canary and Henry Kozicki, eds., *The Writing of History: Literary*

Selected Bibliography

Form and Historical Understanding. Madison: University of Wisconsin Press, 1978. Pp. 129–149.

Morgan, Lewis Henry. *Ancient Society; or, Researches in the Lines of Human Progress from Savagery, through Barbarism to Civilization*. New York, 1877; reprint ed., New York: Meridian Books, 1963.

Neihardt, John G., ed. *Black Elk Speaks*. New York, 1932; reprint ed., Lincoln: University of Nebraska Press, 1979.

O'Brien, Lynne Woods. *Plains Indian Autobiographies*. Boise, Idaho: Boise State College Western Writers Series, 1973.

Ohmann, Richard. "The Shaping of a Canon: U.S. Fiction, 1960–1975," *Critical Inquiry* 10 (September 1983): 199–223.

Ong, Walter J., S.J. *Interfaces of the Word*. Ithaca: Cornell University Press, 1977.

Parsons, Elsie Clews. *American Indian Life*. New York: B. W. Huebsch, 1922; reprint ed., Lincoln: University of Nebraska Press, 1967.

Patterson, J. B. *Black Hawk: An Autobiography*. Edited by Donald Jackson. Urbana: University of Illinois Press, 1964.

Pearce, Roy Harvey. *Savagism and Civilization*. Baltimore: Johns Hopkins Press, 1967.

Prucha, Francis Paul, S.J., ed. *Americanizing the American Indian: Writing by the "Friends of the Indian," 1880–1900*. Cambridge, Mass.: Harvard University Press, 1973.

Quaife, M. M. Introduction to M. M. Quaife, ed., *Kit Carson's Autobiography*. Chicago: Lakeside Press, 1935; reprint ed., Lincoln: University of Nebraska Press, n.d.

Radin, Paul. "The Autobiography of a Winnebago Indian," *University of California Publications in American Archeology and Ethnology* 16 (April 15, 1920): 381–473; reprint ed., New York; Dover, 1963.

———. *Crashing Thunder: The Autobiography of an American Indian*. New York: D. Appleton and Co., 1926; reprint ed., Lincoln: University of Nebraska Press, 1983.

———. "Personal Reminiscences of a Winnebago Indian," *Journal of American Folklore* 26 (1913): 293–318.

———. *Primitive Man as Philosopher*. New York: D. Appleton and Co., 1927.

———. *The Road of Life and Death: A Ritual Drama of the American Indian*. New York: Bollingen-Pantheon, 1945.

────── . *The Winnebago Tribe.* Thirty-Seventh Annual Report of the Bureau of American Ethnology, 1915–1916. Washington, 1923.

Renza, Louis P. "The Veto of the Imagination: A Theory of Autobiography," *New Literary History* 9 (1977): 1–26.

Rothenberg, Jerome, ed. *Shaking the Pumpkin: Traditional Poetry of the Indian North Americas.* Garden City, N.Y.: Doubleday, 1972.

────── , ed. *Technicians of the Sacred: A Range of Poetries from Africa, America, Asia, and Oceania.* Garden City, N.Y.: Doubleday, 1968.

Sabin, Joseph. *Biblioteca Americani: Dictionary of Books Relating to America from its Discovery to the Present Time.* New York, 1868; reprint ed., New York: Mini-Print Corp., n.d.

Said, Edward. *Orientalism.* New York: Vintage Books, 1979.

────── . "The Problem of Textuality: Two Exemplary Positions," *Critical Inquiry* 4 (Summer 1978): 673–714.

────── . "Reflections on Recent American 'Left' Literary Criticism," *Boundary* 2 8 (Fall 1979): 11–30.

Sayre, Robert F. "Vision and Experience in *Black Elk Speaks*," *College English* 32 (1971): 509–535.

Sibbes, Richard. Quoted *in* Perry Miller, *Errand Into the Wilderness.* Cambridge, Mass.: Harvard University Press, 1956.

Simmons, Leo. *Sun Chief: The Autobiography of a Hopi Indian.* New Haven: Yale University Press, 1942.

Slotkin, Richard. *Regeneration Through Violence: The Mythology of the American Frontier, 1600–1860.* Middletown, Conn.: Wesleyan University Press, 1974.

Smith, Henry Nash. *Virgin Land: The American West as Symbol and Myth.* Cambridge, Mass.: Harvard University Press, 1950.

Spivak, Gayatri C. "Revolutions That As Yet Have No Model: Derrida's *Limited Inc,*" *Diacritics* 10 (Winter 1980): 29–49.

Tedlock, Dennis, ed. *Finding the Center: Narrative Poetry of the Zuni Indians.* New York: The Dial Press, 1972; reprint ed., Lincoln: University of Nebraska Press, 1978.

────── . "On the Translation of Style in Oral Narrative," *Journal of American Folklore* 84 (January-March, 1971): 114–133.

────── . "The Spoken Word and the Work of Interpretation." *In* Karl Kroeber, ed., *Traditional American Indian Literatures.* Lincoln: University of Nebraska Press, 1981. Pp. 45–64.

Selected Bibliography

_____ . "Toward an Oral Poetics," *New Literary History* 8 (Spring 1977): 507–519.

Thatcher, B. B. *Indian Biography*. New York, 1832; reprint ed., Glorieta, N.M.: Rio Grande Press, 1973.

Thoreau, Henry David. *Walden and Civil Disobedience*. New York: W. W. Norton, 1966.

Todorov, Tzvetan. *The Fantastic: A Structural Approach to a Literary Genre*. Trans. Richard Howard. Ithaca: Cornell University Press, 1975.

Turner, Frederick W., III. Introduction to *Geronimo: His Own Story*. Edited by S. M. Barrett. New York: Ballantine Books, 1977.

Tyler, Edward B. Quoted *in* A. L. Kroeber and Clyde Kluckhohn, *Culture: A Critical Review of Concepts and Definitions*. New York: Vintage, 1953.

Underhill, Ruth. Foreword to Nancy O. Lurie, ed., *Mountain Wolf Woman: Sister of Crashing Thunder*. Ann Arbor: University of Michigan Press, 1961.

Vestal, Stanley. "The Man Who Killed Custer," *American Heritage* 8 (1957): 4–9, 90–91.

_____ . *Warpath: The True Story of the Fighting Sioux, Told in a Biography of Chief White Bull*. Boston: Houghton Mifflin, 1934.

Watkins, Evan. "Conflict and Consensus in the History of Recent Criticism." *New Literary History* 12 (Winter 1981): 345–365.

White, Hayden. *Metahistory: The Historical Imagination in Nineteenth-Century Europe*. Baltimore: Johns Hopkins Press, 1973.

_____ . "The Historical Text as Literary Artifact." *In* R. H. Canary and Henry Kozicki, eds., *The Writing of History: Literary Form and Historical Understanding*. Madison: University of Wisconsin Press, 1978.

White, Leslie. *The Ethnography and Ethnology of Franz Boas*. Austin Texas Memorial Museum, The Museum of the University of Texas, Bulletin no. 6. Austin, Tex., 1963.

White Bull, Chief Joseph. *The Warrior Who Killed Custer*. Translated and edited by J. H. Howard. Lincoln: University of Nebraska Press, 1968.

Williams, Raymond. *Marxism and Literature*. London: Oxford University Press, 1977.

————. *Problems in Materialism and Culture.* London: Verso Editions, 1980.

Wilson, Gilbert, ed. *Goodbird the Indian.* New York: Fleming H. Revell Co., 1914.

Young, David C. "Crazy Horse on the Trojan Plain: A Comment on the Classicism of John G. Neihardt," *Classical and Modern Literature* 3 (1982): 45–53.

Index

Index

Holland, Norman, 14
Holler, Clyde, 127–134 passim
Horney, Karen, 108
Houston, Sam, 41, 44
Hymes, Dell, 2, 9, 13, 14, 19

imagism, 7
Indian literature: authorship and, 11–16; ceremonies as, 20; changes in attitude toward, 18–23; oral, 3, 19, 42, 119; oratory and, 17; originality and, 11; translation of, 12–13. *See also* translation; canonicity
Indian Removal, 18, 34, 36–40, 44, 54, 115–116
Indian Reorganization Act, 59, 107
Indian, tribes: Cherokee, 18, 30; Cheyenne, 56; Chinook, 19; Chippewa, 19; Chiricahua Apache, 60–74 passim; Creek, 44; Crow, 44; Dakota Sioux, 30; Fox, 44, 45, 48, 50, 72; Hidatsa, 113, 114; Hopi, 109, 114–115; Iroquois, 18; Kwakiutl, 76; Lakota Sioux, 111, 127–136 passim; Lapwai, 116, 124; Mescalero Apache, 71; Nez Perce, 57, 116–126 passim; Nootka, 19; Osage, 20; Papago, 19; Pawnee, 19; Pottawatommie, 103; Quileute, 19; Sac, 44, 45, 48, 50, 72; Seminole, 44; Sioux, 56, 117, 124; Swampy Cree, 12; Takelma, 19; Teton Sioux, 19;

Winnebago, 80–106 passim, 111, 115; Zuni, 12, 18, 19
Indian War Narratives, 35, 37
Iser, Wolfgang, 14

Jackson, President Andrew, 35–36, 38, 41, 42, 45
Jackson, Donald, 46, 69
Jacobs, Melville, 19
Jacobson, Roman, 32
Jameson, Frederic, 9, 15, 23, 26, 74
Jefferson, Thomas, 17
Joseph, Chief, 57–58, 116–118 passim, 125, 126
Joyce, James, 133
Jung, Carl, 92

Kafka, Franz, 130
Kardiner, Abram, 108
Kermode, Frank, 13–14
Kluckhohn, Clyde, 110, 112, 119
Kroeber, Alfred, 18, 65, 76, 83, 84, 85
Kroeber, Karl, 19

La Flesche, Francis, 20
Lame Deer, John (Fire), 134, 136
Langness, L. L., 89
Leavis, F. R., 24
LeClair, Antoine, 45, 47–53, 62
Left-Handed, 112–113, 115
Lester, C. E., 44
Lévi-Strauss, Claude, 2, 22, 108–109

Index

Roosevelt, President Franklin
Delano, 107
Roosevelt, President Theodore,
60
Rothenberg, Jerome, 7, 13, 19,
119
Rousseau, Jean Jacques, 29, 90
Russian Formalists, 119

Said, Edward, 15, 26, 34, 37, 39
Sapir, Edward 18–19, 76, 108
Sartre, Jean Paul, 37
Sayre, Robert, 127
Schoolcraft, Henry, 55, 65
Sequoyah, 30
shaman, 84, 85
Sheperd, Thomas, 40
Sheridan, General Philip, 56
Simmons, Leo, 109, 114
Simms, William Gilmore, 37
Sitting Bull, 56–57, 117, 124
Slotkin, Richard, 39
Smith, William Nash, 54
Southey, Robert, 29
Spivak, Gayatri, 4
Stein, Gertrude, 41
Storm, Hyemeyohsts, 9
Sun Chief. *See* Talayesva, Don

Talayesva, Don, 109, 114–115
Tedlock, Dennis, 3, 6, 12, 13,
19, 119
Thatcher, B. B., 39, 40, 46, 50–
51
Thoreau, Henry, 40, 41, 64
Todorov, Tzvetan, 23, 31
translation, 6, 12–13, 81
Turner, Frederick Jackson, 73
Turner, Frederick W., 61, 67

Underhill, Ruth, 89, 92, 105,
126

Virgil, 129
Voltaire, 93, 122

Wheeler-Howard Act. *See* Indian
Reorganization Act
White, Hayden, 49, 66
White, Leslie, 72, 78
Williams, Raymond, 14, 15, 20,
24, 26
Williams, William Carlos, 121
Wilson, Gilbert, 113
Wordsworth, William, 17
Wounded Knee, 127, 132

Yellow Wolf, 116–126

Designer:	Cynthia Krupat
Compositor:	Publisher's Typography
Printer:	Edwards Bros.
Binder:	Edwards Bros.
Text:	Electra
Display:	Electra